Maxims

La Rochefoucauld

Translation, introduction, and notes by
Stuart D. Warner and
Stéphane Douard

ST. AUGUSTINE'S PRESS
South Bend, Indiana
2001

Manufactured in the United States of America.

1 2 3 4 5 6   07 06 05 04 03 02 01

Library of Congress Cataloging in Publication Data
La Rochefoucauld, François, duc de, 1613–1680.
    [Maximes. English]
    Maxims / La Rochefoucauld; translation, introduction and notes
    by Stuart D. Warner and Stéphane Douard.
        p.   cm.
    Includes bibliographical references and index.
    ISBN 1-890318-42-6
    1. Maxims. I. Warner, Stuart D., 1955– II. Douard, Stéphane,
    1969– III. Title.
PQ1815 .A72 2001
848'.402 - dc21   2001000507

∞ *The paper used in this publication meets the minimum requirements of the American
National Standard for Information Sciences – Permanence of Paper for Printed
Materials, ANSI Z39.48-1984.*

Contents

Introduction

"La Rochefoucauld and those other French masters in examining the soul . . . resemble skillful marksmen who hit the bull's eye again and again – the bull's eye of human nature. Their skill arouses amazement. But a spectator who is guided not by the spirit of science, but by the spirit of philanthropy, finally curses an art that seems to plant a sense of suspicion and diminishment in the souls of men."

Nietzsche, *Human, All Too Human*, sec. 36

François VI de La Rochefoucauld (1613–1680), a courtier and a soldier, first presented his intricate masterpiece to the world in 1665. The *Réflexions ou sentences et maximes morales* went through several editions, culminating in the authoritative fifth edition of 1678, an edition substantially longer than any of the others.

Throughout the English-speaking world – and the French, as well – the work is simply called the *Maxims*, a title markedly more simple than the one which La Rochefoucauld actually bestowed upon his work. Such simplicity, however, diverts the attention of the reader away from the diffuse and complex meaning of the complete title – possibly concealing something essential to La Rochefoucauld's intention – even before the reader attends to the body of the work itself.

We can at least begin to think about what is truly an elusive and ambiguous title by noticing how strongly it resists a literal translation into English. *Réflexions ou sentences et maximes morales* consists of three nouns – *réflexions*, *sentences*, and *maximes* – two conjunctions – *ou* and *et* – and one adjective – *morales*. We can render the nouns as *reflections*, *judgments*, and *maxims*, respectively, the conjunctions as *or* and *and*, and the adjective as *moral*. One thing which the French makes unclear is the scope of application of the adjective and both conjunctions. Is it *Moral Reflections* or simply *Reflections*, for example? However one decides that, is it *Moral Reflections or Moral Judgments and Moral Maxims*, or is it *Moral Reflections or Moral Judgments and Moral Maxims*?

Obviously, critical to understanding the title are the meanings of *réflexions*, *sentences*, and *maximes*. *Sentences* and *maximes* are close to each other in meaning, but not identical. Both refer to statements which are brief. *Sentences* is at home in a juridical context, often referring to a judgment about a person's guilt or innocence, but it is also used more simply in the sense of judgment or opinion. *Maximes* is at home in a moral or theological context, often in the form of a general proposition enunciating some principle or rule.[1] Of these three general terms, *réflexions* stands most apart from the others, referring as it does to a longer, more elaborate thought or argument. In La Rochefoucauld's book, there are at least two types of *reflections*: first, those lengthy so-called maxims – for example, the last one, which is on death (504), or an earlier one on valor and cowardice (215); and second, those clusters of maxims (or judgments) which offer a series of thoughts, taking up a subject first from one perspective and then another – for example, the early cluster on passion (5–12) or the cluster on praise (143–50). These longer reflections and clusters appear to be of a somewhat different breed from the succinct, more abbreviated, and seemingly unconnected maxims (or judgments).

There is another sense – *the* most important sense – of *réflexions* at play in the *Réflexions ou sentences et maximes morales*, and one way of beginning to think about this is to turn to a signal difference

1   See La Bruyère, *Les Caractères*, Preface, toward the end.

between Montaigne and La Rochefoucauld. In his *Essays* (1580–88), Montaigne refers to himself – *I*, *me*, *mine*, and *my* – over six thousand times.[2] Just as remarkably, La Rochefoucauld refers to himself only five times – three of these occurring in the final reflection on death, and one of the other two in the next longest single reflection (233). Montaigne offers an understanding of the human condition mediated by an understanding of himself; and this is intimately connected in the *Essays* to his valorizing the activity of self-examination.[3] For La Rochefoucauld, it is primarily by observing in others the characteristics of being human that an individual is able to recognize these characteristics in himself, and thereby achieve if only limited self-knowledge. His work, which exhibits a pronounced skepticism about the veracity of claims of self-knowledge,[4] has us begin with others and only then make the turn to ourselves. In this manner, others serve as a *mirror*, and our understanding of ourselves as human is thus mediated by seeing ourselves as a *reflection* of others.

However, because the desire for self-knowledge, as La Rochefoucauld conceives of it, is not particularly strong in human beings, this process does not come so naturally. Thus, La Rochefoucauld attempts to structure his book so as gradually to lead his readers to direct their gaze within; and he intends to bring this result about through the wit, sharpness, condescension, and bluntness of the book. Readers are seduced into thinking that they are laughing at others, seeing the folly of others, taking pleasure in the misbegotten deeds of others, and being amazed at the extent and variety of acts of dissimulation practiced by others. However, the *others* are no different from *oneself*. By touching on so many aspects of being human, La Rochefoucauld aims to induce a *gestalt*-like

---

2   See Roy E. Leake, ed., *Concordance des Essais de Montaigne* (Genève: Librairie Droz, 1981).

3   Compare Hobbes, *Leviathan*, The Introduction, toward the end.

4   See, for example, 36, 42, 69, 106, 114, 295, 458, and 460.

experience (or switch) in his readers. To the extent that one more and more recognizes oneself in others, a transferral takes place, and one realizes that one has been witnessing one's own shortcomings. Affected by the immediacy of this newfound understanding of oneself, the possibility of greater self-awareness, and, therefore, greater prospects for self-knowledge, comes to exist.

Here we come to see the most vital sense of *réflexions*. La Rochefoucauld's book itself is a series of mirrors, which, by affording us the possibility of observing human beings generally, affords us the possibility of knowing ourselves. Each "maxim" is a *reflection* in this sense. And perhaps it is precisely this sense that La Rochefoucauld has foremost in mind when he places the words *REFLEXIONS MORALES* at the head of the opening page of the *Réflexions ou sentences et maximes morales*. By averting its gaze from any particular individual, the book is able to offer an image of things human through which we can acquire a deeper understanding of ourselves as individuals.

La Rochefoucauld's theme of the hiddenness of individuals from themselves – hence the difficult if not near-insurmountable obstacles to self-knowledge – is connected to the broader theme that literally frames his work as a whole: the problem of appearance and reality. This problem itself is presented through the spectacles of virtue and vice, and it first comes to our attention in the epigraph to the work: "Our virtues are, most often, only vices disguised." Throughout, La Rochefoucauld presents a litany of examples testifying to just this: what appear to be virtues and marks of excellence are only apparently so, for the motives guiding them are associated more with vice than with virtue. The purity of motive required for true virtue is rare. Thus, sincerity is ordinarily an act of dissimulation to win over others (62); the love of justice for most involves the fear of suffering injustice (78); generosity is often a disguised ambition (246); fidelity in most people flows from self-love (247); liberality is most often vanity in action (263); magnanimity is the most noble means of receiving praise (285); great and brilliant actions are not ordinarily the effects of great designs but of the humors and passions (7). Yet, La Rochefoucauld believes that the truth to which these examples point is but little recognized, and this indeed reveals the human penchant for conflating the appearances of things with the realities themselves.[5] Thus, those who act in a manner which appears just often believe themselves to be acting justly; and those who witness such actions ordinarily believe themselves to be in the presence of the just. Actors and spectators alike are misled.[6]

This, for La Rochefoucauld, is not a problem owing to the circumstances of the times – it flows from the permanent condition of human beings. Ultimately, this condition springs from the array of passions which principally govern men and women, and not reason. Over these passions we have but little control; they move us and, alas, they blind us.[7] Self-love, interest, jealousy, envy, vanity, avarice, pride, the love of praise, flattery, laziness, timidity – these reign in the realm of things human; and although self-love occupies an important place here, its importance to La Rochefoucauld's thought is usually overrated.[8] At every turn, his interest lies in delineating the intricate and tangled web of motives which underlie and inform human conduct.

La Rochefoucauld's manner of thought here becomes even more visible when seen in the light of one of his most frequently *misquoted* maxims. He is reported to have written that "hypocrisy is *the* homage vice pays to virtue." Instead, what he does write is that "hypocrisy is *an* homage vice pays to virtue" (218; our emphases). What he is suggesting is that there are various instances of vice's

5   See 302.
6   See 409.
7   See, for example, 5, 10, and 102.
8   Some of this is, we believe, due to the fact the first edition of the *Réflexions ou sentences et maximes morales* began with a lengthy reflection on self-love. This reflection only appeared in the first edition. In our edition it is the first of the

paying homage to virtue, and hypocrisy is but one of these.[9] The reader is thus invited to reflect on what these other instances might be. In part, what is striking here is La Rochefoucauld's enthusiastic embrace of the multiplicity of things. However, La Rochefoucauld's capacious mind leads to his embracing something quite different as well, namely, the enterprise of combining elements that do not obviously go together, or whose connection is difficult to see, at least at first blush. One way in which he proceeds along these lines is when he follows a *semi-colon* with an *and*, a syntax he uses in over forty "maxims," and which seems too innocuous even to mention. However, what this allows him to do is to end a thought, and then, almost as an afterthought, to add something on that is crucial, some pivotal relationship, which is often the central point of the "maxim."

Deeply connected to La Rochefoucauld's understanding of the power of the passions is his understanding of the commanding influence of fortune, both as a cosmic agency and as a determining element in the domain of things human.[10] Thus, whereas fortune appears in nearly thirty of the "maxims," God does not make so much as a single appearance.[11] Here is a fragmented and unsteady universe in which passion and fortune have a primacy which reason and providence simply lack; and as a consequence of this, the capacity that the majority of individuals have to affect their lives appears severely compromised.[12]

However bleak La Rochefoucauld's outlook may be, it is important to realize that it is tempered by the recognition that at least some human beings are capable of greatness. Although "nothing is rarer than true goodness" (481), such goodness or virtue is in

---

"withdrawn maxims." However, compare Leo Strauss, *The Political Philosophy of Hobbes* (Oxford: the Clarendon Press, 1936), p. xiv.

9   See 233.

10   See 435.

11   230, 341, and 358 must be considered in this regard.

12   Compare Machiavelli, *The Prince*, ch. 25.

13   See, for example, 62, 95, 157, 160, 215, 376, 399, and 473.

point of fact to be found.[13] As one examines the myriad of such cases in which virtue is shown to be a vice disguised, one finds that La Rochefoucauld almost always manages to record that this is "ordinarily" or "for the most part" the case, and not always so. Although greatness or excellence or merit do not belong to the common lot of things, such is the human disposition that we delude ourselves into thinking that they are. Consequently, we issue a currency that is counterfeit, in which appearances or mere words replace the reality of things. Thus, at the heart of the *Réflexions ou sentences et maximes morales* lies the attempt to disclose the great disparity that exists between the exaggerated self-estimation of men and women and their actual condition.

It is within the trajectory of this understanding that one of La Rochefoucauld's most beautiful and trenchant maxims must be understood: "Virtues lose themselves in self-interest, as rivers lose themselves in the sea" (171). The meaning which is critical here is that just as rivers are swallowed up by the sea, the sea's being so much larger, so virtues are dwarfed by self-interest, because the latter is vastly more common. This maxim allows us to recognize that while apparent virtues are many, virtue proper is hard to discern because of what surrounds it. Nonetheless, it must be added that there is another meaning to this maxim – one almost completely different from the first! Just as rivers cease being rivers when swallowed up by the sea, and thereby become one with the sea, so virtues are transformed by self-interest and become one with it, thereby ceasing to be virtues. This duality of being one yet two seems to point both to the resistance of reality to categorization and the astonishing capacity of language to represent reality in manifold ways.[14]

In effect, La Rochefoucauld holds up a prism in front of his mind's eye, and it is through this prism that he views the vast panorama of the human condition. Human beings appear as frail

14   See 12.

and fragmentary, as an assemblage of fluctuating parts, parts which are always in motion.[15]

We are also beings for whom dissimulation is a matter of course. Thus, with our own interests of paramount importance in almost whatever we do, we practice the arts of deception, aiming to become masters of the world of appearances which we ourselves hope to generate, a world in which our own interests can best be satisfied.[16] La Rochefoucauld takes some pains to try to make known how this animates and degrades human relationships, especially the most intimate human relationships, those of love and friendship.[17] The bitter invective which he unleashes upon these matters is unmatched anywhere else in the book, but it is modulated by a certain playfulness and humor — one does not know sometimes whether to laugh or to cry, or both — and one is led to recognize the strange qualities of love and friendship as La Rochefoucauld paints them in all of their tragic and comic dimensions.

It is all the more remarkable that in the face of La Rochefoucauld's persistent endeavors to reveal the constant motion that pervades human life, he should conclude and anchor the book in the very obverse of that motion itself, namely, death. This lengthy reflection, more than three times longer than any other one in the 1678 edition, serves as the conclusion to every edition of the *Réflexions ou sentences et maximes morales*.[18] The finality and fixedness of its place match the finality and fixedness of its subject. Death is that to which all life points and the point at which it ends. It is true north on the compass of life.

15 See 10.

16 See 501.

17 The most extensive cluster of maxims or judgments (68–88) considers love and friendship. This theme, also, is given a good deal of attention toward the end of the *Réflexions ou sentences et maximes morales*. It is toward the end of the work that one finds most of the maxims about women.

18 In the first edition, it was unnumbered, serving perhaps as a pendant for the work as a whole. Also, there are some variants in this reflection from edition to edition, but its essential character remains the same throughout.

La Rochefoucauld's treatment of death in his final reflection is similar to his treatment of "apparent virtues." The falseness or appearance which occupies him here is the *contempt* for death. The Pagans, he says, boast of a contempt drawn from their own resources, a contempt which brazenly presents death as something other than an evil. However, it is "the greatest of all evils,"[19] and La Rochefoucauld avows that no one "with good sense ever believed" death to be anything other than an evil. "Any man who knows how to see it as it is finds that it is a dreadful thing." In the face of the necessity of death, remedies suggest themselves. Philosophers, as well as others, conceive of creating an eternal reputation; some think of being regretted long after they are gone; still others point to a newfound freedom from the whims of fortune.[20] Strikingly, these are remedies only insofar as they divert our attention from knowing or imagining death "in all of its particulars." But these are not infallible, for the closer we get to death, the more it arrests our attention, and the more such remedies begin to fail. The best we can do is to look away from death and to rest our sight upon other things. La Rochefoucauld fails to discuss the consequences of attending to death in all of its details, but the inference is clear: the pleasures which life offers will be replaced by an impenetrable fog of insipid gloominess. At the end of the day, withdrawing our attention from the *reality* of life's end is the price one must pay for the enjoyment of life itself. "Neither the sun," that is, life, "nor death can be looked at steadily" (26).[21]

La Rochefoucauld's *Réflexions ou sentences et maximes morales* are serious, yet they are playful and ironic; and while beautiful for the eye and ear, they are also blunt and always bold. Worthy of study at all times, they are perhaps especially weighty during those moments when the mask has come to be the face itself; when appearance alone

19 See 503.

20 Compare Boethius, *The Consolation of Philosophy*, I.6.17.

21 Compare Plato, *Phaedo* 99d–e.

reigns while reality flounders; when darkness appears to obscure all. There is one occasion in his masterpiece when La Rochefoucauld plainly throws aside whatever mask *he* may be wearing, and offers a confident statement of the manner in which he proceeds: "As it is the character of great minds to make many things understood with few words, so small minds, to the contrary, have the gift of talking a lot and of saying nothing" (142). His extraordinary economy of language might tempt us into conflating it with shortsightedness of thought. Nietzsche reminds us that that is a temptation which we should resist.

Translators' Note

The present translation attempts to render La Rochefoucauld's *Réflexions ou sentences et maximes morales* into English as literally as possible consistent with readability and intelligibility. Toward this end, we directed our efforts to rendering the key words used in the original French by the same English words throughout. Our desire to be literal also extended to word order of the *Maxims*, since we believe that that order is often important to understanding La Rochefoucauld's intention.

We have tried to reproduce La Rochefoucauld's eloquence, but we have been willing to sacrifice it – albeit grudgingly – for the sake of accuracy and clarity of meaning. We believe that our author has arresting and penetrating things to say about the human condition, and our translation aims to make those things apparent.

Our English translation attempts to parallel the clarity and readability of La Rochefoucauld's original French. When we thought that the French was intentionally deceptive and thus difficult to understand, we did not try to simplify the English in the hope of unveiling La Rochefoucauld's meaning. Furthermore, there are times when a maxim is almost symmetrical, but not quite – and in those cases we did not make it more symmetrical in English than it is in the French.

Because almost all of the *Maxims* are short, it is tempting to believe that they must be readily and easily understandable. Our own experience is that this is far from true, and that sometimes one has to puzzle over them to grasp the twist or turn or irony which, when in hand, makes them clearer.

The five hundred and four maxims which constitute the authoritative fifth edition of the *Maxims* provide the heart of our work. There are two other sets of "maxims" that have been customarily appended to this 1678 edition of *Maxims*, and we have followed this custom and included them in our edition. First is the *Withdrawn Maxims*, and it contains maxims which La Rochefoucauld published in one of the four earlier editions but did not include in the fifth. The second is the so-called *Posthumous Maxims*, and it is drawn from several sources. These latter maxims must be used with some caution, since in many cases their authorship is in doubt, and in all cases there is little if any evidence that La Rochefoucauld thought that they should be published as part of the *Maxims*. In addition to the various maxims, we have included three portraits, two written by La Rochefoucauld and one written about him.

We used the original 1678 edition of the *Réflexions ou sentences et maximes morales* (which one of us has the pleasure to own) as our copytext. We used two major French editions of La Rochefoucauld for the other texts translated in this work. The first is *Œuvres de La Rochefoucauld*, edited by M.D.L. Gilbert, J. Gourdault, A. Régnier, and H. Régnier, in four volumes, which is in the wonderful *Collection des Grands Ecrivains de la France* series. The second is the edition of La Rochefoucauld's writings edited by Jacques Truchet. Truchet's edition – *un modèle du genre* – is the work to which one must first turn for any scholarly questions about the French text.

The French dictionaries of Emile Littré and Paul Robert were always close at hand, and we were never without *Harrap's New Standard French and English Dictionary*; also, the seventeenth- and eighteenth-century French dictionaries which the ARTFL project at the University of Chicago makes available were very useful, indeed. Finally, we should mention a rather forgotten book upon which we relied more than once: James Fernald's dictionary of synonyms and antonyms.

The image on the cover of this edition reproduces the frontispiece which graced the first four editions of the *Maxims*.

We need to acknowledge special debts to three people. Samuel Lester checked the translation of a good number of the more difficult maxims and always offered sage advice. Lisa M. Kaderabek was indispensable in examining our English versions and finding infelicities which even now make us blanch. Lastly, Bruce Fingerhut showed us that patience is not always a vice disguised, and if only for that we are grateful. We could not have found a better and more sympathetic publisher.

Le libraire au lecteur

Cette cinquième édition des Réflexions morales est augmentée de plus de cent nouvelles maximes, et plus exacte que les quatre premières. L'approbation que le public leur a donnée est au-dessus de ce que je puis dire en leur faveur. Et si elles sont telles que je les crois, comme j'ai sujet d'en être persuadé, on ne pourrait leur faire plus de tort que de s'imaginer qu'elles eussent besoin d'apologie. Je me contenterai de vous avertir de deux choses: l'une, que par le mot d'*Intérêt*, on n'entend pas toujours un intérêt de bien, mais le plus souvent un intérêt d'honneur ou de gloire; et l'autre (qui est comme le fondement de toutes ces réflexions), que celui qui les a faites n'a considéré les hommes que dans cet état déplorable de la nature corrompue par le péché; et qu'ainsi la manière dont il parle de ce nombre infini de défauts qui se rencontrent dans leurs vertus apparentes ne regarde point ceux que Dieu en préserve par une grâce particulière.

Pour ce qui est de l'ordre de ces réflexions, on n'aura pas de peine à juger que comme elles sont toutes sur des matières différentes, il était difficile d'y en observer. Et bien qu'il y en ait plusieurs sur un même sujet, on n'a pas cru les devoir toujours mettre de suite, de crainte d'ennuyer le lecteur; mais on les trouvera dans la table.

The Bookseller to the Reader[1]

This fifth edition of the *Moral Reflections* is increased by more than one hundred new maxims, and it is more exact than the first four editions. The approbation the public has given them is beyond whatever I could say in their favor; and if they are as I believe them to be – and I have reason to be persuaded of this – one could not do a greater wrong to them than to suppose that they needed an apology. I shall be content with warning you about two things. The first is that the word *Interêt* does not always mean the interest concerned with material goods, but most often means the interest concerned with glory or honor. The second (which is as the ground of all of these reflections) is that he who has made these reflections has only considered men in that deplorable state of nature corrupted by sin; and, thus, the manner in which he speaks of this infinite number of shortcomings which are found in their apparent virtues, does not pertain to those men God shields from these shortcomings by a particular grace.

With regard to what the order of these reflections is, one will have no difficulty judging that, as they all are about different subject matters, it was difficult to observe any order in them. And although several are about the same subject, we did not believe we always had to put them together for fear of boring the reader; but one will find them in the index.

---

1   This note was written by La Rochefoucauld in the character of a bookseller, and it served as a "Preface" to the fifth edition of the *Maxims*.

Moral Reflections

Nos vertus ne sont, le plus souvent, que des vices déguisés.
Our virtues are, most often, only vices disguised.

1 *Ce que nous prenons pour des vertus n'est souvent qu'un assemblage de diverses actions et de divers intérêts, que la fortune ou notre industrie savent arranger; et ce n'est pas toujours par valeur et par chasteté que les hommes sont vaillants, et que les femmes sont chastes.*
What we take for virtues are often only a collection of various actions and interests which fortune or our own industry knows how to arrange; and it is not always through valor and chastity that men are valiant and that women are chaste.

2 *L'amour-propre est le plus grand de tous les flatteurs.*
Self-love is the greatest of all flatterers.

3 *Quelque découverte que l'on ait faite dans le pays l'amour-propre, il y reste encore bien des terres inconnues.*
Whatever discovery was made in the country of self-love, many unknown lands remain there still.

4 *L'amour-propre est plus habile que le plus habile homme du monde.*
Self-love is more clever than the most clever man in the world.

5 *La durée de nos passions ne dépend pas plus de nous que la durée de notre vie.*

5   The duration of our passions depends on us no more than the duration of our lives.

6   *La passion fait souvent un fou du plus habile homme, et rend souvent les plus sots habiles.*
Passion often makes a madman out of the most clever man, and often renders the most foolish clever.

7   *Ces grandes et éclatantes actions qui éblouissent les yeux sont représentées par les politiques comme les effets des grands desseins, au lieu que ce sont d'ordinaire les effets de l'humeur et des passions. Ainsi la guerre d'Auguste et d'Antoine, qu'on rapporte à l'ambition qu'ils avaient de se rendre maîtres du monde, n'était peut-être qu'un effet de jalousie.*
These great and brilliant actions which dazzle the eyes are represented by statesmen as the effects of great designs, whereas they are ordinarily the effects of the humors and of the passions. Thus, the war of Augustus and Anthony, which is ascribed to the ambition they had to become masters of the world, was perhaps only an effect of jealousy.

8   *Les passions sont les seuls orateurs qui persuadent toujours. Elles sont comme un art de la nature dont les règles sont infaillibles; et l'homme le plus simple qui a de la passion persuade mieux que le plus éloquent qui n'en a point.*
Passions are the only orators which always persuade. They are like an art of nature, the rules of which are infallible; and the simplest man who has some passion persuades better than the most eloquent who has none.

9   *Les passions ont une injustice et un propre intérêt qui fait qu'il est dangereux de les suivre, et qu'on s'en doit défier lors même qu'elles paraissent les plus raisonnables.*

9   Passions have an injustice and a self-interest of their own which makes following them dangerous, and one should distrust them, even when they appear most reasonable.

10   *Il y a dans le cœur humain une génération perpétuelle de passions, en sorte que la ruine de l'une est presque toujours l'établissement d'une autre.*

There is in the human heart a perpetual generation of passions, such that the downfall of one is almost always the establishment of another.

11   *Les passions en engendrent souvent qui leur sont contraires. L'avarice produit quelquefois la prodigalité; et la prodigalité l'avarice; on est souvent ferme par faiblesse, et audacieux par timidité.*

Passions often engender passions which are contrary to them. Avarice sometimes begets prodigality, and prodigality avarice; one is often resolute through weakness, and bold through timidity.

12   *Quelque soin que l'on prenne de couvrir ses passions par des apparences de piété et d'honneur, elles paraissent toujours au travers de ces voiles.*

Whatever care one takes to cover one's passions with appearances of piety and honor, they always appear through these veils.

13   *Notre amour-propre souffre plus impatiemment la condamnation de nos goûts que de nos opinions.*

Our self-love suffers more impatiently the condemnation of our tastes than our opinions.

14   *Les hommes ne sont pas seulement sujets à perdre le souvenir des bienfaits et des injures; ils haïssent même ceux qui les ont obligés, et cessent*

ceux qui leur ont fait des outrages. L'application à récompenser
, et à se venger du mal, leur paraît une servitude à laquelle ils
eine de se soumettre.

n are not only subject to losing the memory of benefits and injuries, they even hate those who benefited them, and cease to hate those who have committed outrages against them. The diligence of rewarding the good and taking revenge on the bad appears to them as a servitude into which they have difficulty delivering themselves.

15 *La clémence des princes n'est souvent qu'une politique pour gagner l'affection des peuples.*
The leniency of princes is often only a policy for winning the affection of the people.

16 *Cette clémence dont on fait une vertu se pratique tantôt par vanité, quelquefois par paresse, souvent par crainte, et presque toujours par tous les trois ensemble.*
This leniency of which a virtue is made is sometimes practiced out of vanity, now and then out of laziness, often out of fear, and almost always out of all three together.

17 *La modération des personnes heureuses vient du calme que la bonne fortune donne à leur humeur.*
The moderation of happy people comes from the calm that good fortune gives to their humors.

18 *La modération est une crainte de tomber dans l'envie et dans le mépris que méritent ceux qui s'enivrent de leur bonheur; c'est une vaine ostentation de la force de notre esprit; et enfin la modération des hommes dans leur plus haute élévation est un désir de paraître plus grands que leur fortune.*
Moderation is a fear of falling into the envy and contempt

deserved by those who become intoxicated with their happiness; it is a vain display of the strength of our spirit; and finally the moderation of men at their highest height is a desire to appear greater than their fortune.

19 *Nous avons tous assez de force pour supporter les maux d'autrui.*
We all have strength enough to endure the pains of others.

20 *La constance des sages n'est que l'art de renfermer leur agitation dans leur cœur.*
The constancy of the wise is only the art of containing their agitation in their hearts.

21 *Ceux qu'on condamne au supplice affectent quelquefois une constance et un mépris de la mort qui n'est en effet que la crainte de l'envisage., De sorte qu'on peut dire que cette constance et ce mépris sont à leur esprit ce que le bandeau est à leurs yeux.*
Those who are condemned to the rack sometimes affect a constancy and a contempt of death which is in fact only the fear of facing it; so that one could say that this constancy and contempt are to their spirit what a blindfold is to their eyes.

22 *La philosophie triomphe aisément des maux passés et des maux à venir. Mais les maux présents triomphent d'elle.*
Philosophy triumphs easily over the ills of the past and the ills to come, but present ills triumph over her.

23 *Peu de gens connaissent la mort. On ne la souffre pas ordinairement par résolution, mais par stupidité et par coutume; et la plupart des hommes meurent parce qu'on ne peut s'empêcher de mourir.*
Few people know death. One does not ordinarily endure it through resolve, but through stupidity and custom; most men die because they cannot prevent themselves from dying.

24 *Lorsque les grands hommes se laissent abattre par la longueur de leurs infortunes, ils font voir qu'ils ne les soutenaient que par la force de leur ambition, et non par celle de leur âme, et qu'à une grande vanité près les héros sont faits comme les autres hommes.*

When great men let themselves be disheartened by the extent of their misfortunes, they reveal that they withstood them only through the strength of their ambition, and not through that of their soul; and that except for great vanity, heroes are made like other men.

25 *Il faut de plus grandes vertus pour soutenir la bonne fortune que la mauvaise.*

One needs greater virtues to hold out against good fortune than bad.

26 *Le soleil ni la mort ne se peuvent regarder fixement.*

Neither the sun nor death can be looked at steadily.

27 *On fait souvent vanité des passions même les plus criminelles; mais l'envie est une passion timide et honteuse que l'on n'ose jamais avouer.*

One often prides oneself on even the most criminal passions; but envy is a timid and shameful passion which one never dares confess.

28 *La jalousie est en quelque manière juste et raisonnable, puisqu'elle ne tend qu'à conserver un bien qui nous appartient, ou que nous croyons nous appartenir; au lieu que l'envie est une fureur qui ne peut souffrir le bien des autres.*

Jealousy is in some manner just and reasonable, since it only aims at preserving a good which belongs to us or which we believe belongs to us, whereas envy is a fury which cannot bear the good of others.

29 *Le mal que nous faisons ne nous attire pas tant de persécution et de haine que nos bonnes qualités.*
The evil we do does not bring upon us as much persecution and hatred as our good qualities.

30 *Nous avons plus de force que de volonté; et c'est souvent pour nous excuser à nous-mêmes que nous nous imaginons que les choses sont impossibles.*
We have more strength than will; and it is often in order to excuse ourselves that we imagine that things are impossible.

31 *Si nous n'avions point de défauts, nous ne prendrions pas tant de plaisir à en remarquer dans les autres.*
If we did not have any shortcomings, we would not enjoy noticing them in others so much.

32 *La jalousie se nourrit dans les doutes et elle devient fureur, ou elle finit, sitôt qu'on passe du doute à la certitude.*
Jealousy feeds upon doubts and she turns into fury, or she ends as soon as one passes from doubt to certitude.

33 *L'orgueil se dédommage toujours et ne perd rien lors même qu'il renonce à la vanité.*
Pride always compensates itself and loses nothing even when it renounces vanity.

34 *Si nous n'avions point d'orgueil, nous ne nous plaindrions pas de celui des autres.*
If we did not have pride, we would not complain of it in others.

35 *L'orgueil est égal dans tous les hommes, et il n'y a de différence qu'aux moyens et à la manière de le mettre au jour.*

35 Pride is equal in all men, and there is a difference only in the means and manner of bringing it into the light of day.

36 *Il semble que la nature, qui a si sagement disposé les organes de notre corps pour nous rendre heureux, nous ait aussi donné l'orgueil pour nous épargner la douleur de connaître nos imperfections.*
It seems that nature, which has so wisely ordered the organs of our body to make us happy, also gave us pride to spare us the pain of knowing our imperfections.

37 *L'orgueil a plus de part que la bonté aux remontrances que nous faisons à ceux qui commettent des fautes; et nous ne les reprenons pas tant pour les en corriger que pour leur persuader que nous en sommes exempts.*
Pride plays a greater part than goodness in the objections we make to those who commit mistakes; and we admonish them not so much to correct them as to convince them that we are exempt from these mistakes.

38 *Nous promettons selon nos espérances, et nous tenons selon nos craintes.*
We make promises according to our hopes, and we keep them according to our fears.

39 *L'intérêt parle toutes sortes de langues, et joue toutes sortes de personnages, même celui de désintéressé.*
Self-interest speaks all manner of tongues and plays all manner of roles, even that of the disinterested.

40 *L'intérêt, qui aveugle les uns, fait la lumière des autres.*
Self-interest, which blinds some, brings enlightenment to others.

41 *Ceux qui s'appliquent trop aux petites choses deviennent ordinairement incapables des grandes.*

41 Those who apply themselves too much to small things ordinarily become incapable of great ones.

42 *Nous n'avons pas assez de force pour suivre toute notre raison.*
We do not have enough strength to follow wholly our reason.

43 *L'homme croit souvent se conduire lorsqu'il est conduit; et pendant que par son esprit il tend à un but, son cœur l'entraîne insensiblement à un autre.*
Man often believes he leads when he is being led; and while his mind tends toward one end, his heart insensibly draws him toward another.

44 *La force et la faiblesse de l'esprit sont mal nommées; elles ne sont en effet que la bonne ou la mauvaise disposition des organes du corps.*
Strength and weakness of the mind are poorly named; they are indeed only the good or bad condition of the organs of the body.

45 *Le caprice de notre humeur est encore plus bizarre que celui de la fortune.*
The capriciousness of our humors is even more bizarre than that of fortune.

46 *L'attachement ou l'indifférence que les philosophes avaient pour la vie n'était qu'un goût de leur amour-propre, dont on ne doit non plus disputer que du goût de la langue ou du choix des couleurs.*
The fondness or the indifference which philosophers had for life was only a taste of their self-love, which should not be disputed anymore than the choice of language or the choice of colours.

47 *Notre humeur met le prix à tout ce qui nous vient de la fortune.*
Our humors set the price on all that comes to us from fortune.

48 *La félicité est dans le goût et non pas dans les choses; et c'est par avoir ce qu'on aime qu'on est heureux, et non par avoir ce que les autres trouvent aimable.*

Felicity is in taste and not in things; and it is by having what one loves that one is happy, and not by having what others find agreeable.

49 *On n'est jamais si heureux ni si malheureux qu'on s'imagine.*

One is never so happy or so unhappy as one imagines.

50 *Ceux qui croient avoir du mérite se font un honneur d'être malheureux, pour persuader aux autres et à eux-mêmes qu'ils sont dignes d'être en butte à la fortune.*

Those who believe they have merit pride themselves on being unhappy to persuade others and themselves that they are worthy of being exposed to fortune.

51 *Rien ne doit tant diminuer la satisfaction que nous avons de nous-mêmes, que de voir que nous désapprouvons dans un temps ce que nous approuvions dans un autre.*

Nothing should diminish the satisfaction we take in ourselves so much as seeing that what we disapprove of at one time we approve of at another.

52 *Quelque différence qui paraisse entre les fortunes, il y a néanmoins une certaine compensation de biens et de maux qui les rend égales.*

Whatever difference there may seem to be among fortunes, there is nevertheless a certain compensation of good and bad which renders them equal.

53 *Quelques grands advantages que la nature donne, ce n'est pas elle seule, mais la fortune avec elle qui fait les héros.*

53   However great the advantages which nature gives, it is not her alone, but fortune with her, which makes heroes.

54   *Le mépris des richesses était dans les philosophes un désir caché de venger leur mérite de l'injustice de la fortune par le mépris des mêmes biens dont elle les privait; c'était un secret pour se garantir de l'avilissement de la pauvreté; c'était un chemin détourné pour aller à la considération qu'ils ne pouvaient avoir par les richesses.*
Among the philosophers, contempt for wealth was a hidden desire to avenge their merit against the injustice of fortune by the contempt of the very goods of which fortune deprived them; it was a secret to protect themselves from the debasement of poverty; it was an indirect way of acquiring the esteem they could not have from wealth.

55   *La haine pour les favoris n'est autre chose que l'amour de la faveur. Le dépit de ne la pas posséder se console et s'adoucit par le mépris que l'on témoigne de ceux qui la possèdent; et nous leur refusons nos hommages, ne pouvant pas leur ôter ce qui leur attire ceux de tout le monde.*
The hatred for favorites is nothing but the love of favor. The vexation of not being favored is consoled and softened by the contempt we display to those who are; and we refuse them our respect, unable as we are to take away what brings them the respect of everyone else.

56   *Pour s'établir dans le monde, on fait tout ce que l'on peut pour y paraître établi.*
In order to establish oneself in the world, one does everything one can to appear established in it.

57   *Quoique les hommes se flattent de leurs grandes actions, elles ne sont pas souvent les effets d'un grand dessein, mais des effets du hasard.*

57 Although men flatter themselves on their great actions, these are seldom the effect of a great design, but the effect of chance.

58 *Il semble que nos actions aient des étoiles heureuses ou malheureuses à qui elles doivent une grande partie de la louange et du blâme qu'on leur donne.*
It seems that our actions have lucky or unlucky stars to which they owe a great deal of the praise and the blame which one bestows upon them.

59 *Il n'y a point d'accidents si malheureux dont les habiles gens ne tirent quelque avantage, ni de si heureux que les imprudents ne puissent tourner à leur préjudice.*
There is no accident so unfortunate that clever people do not draw some advantage from it, or any so fortunate that the imprudent cannot turn it to their detriment.

60 *La fortune tourne tout à l'avantage de ceux qu'elle favorise.*
Fortune turns everything to the advantage of those she favors.

61 *Le bonheur et le malheur des hommes ne dépend pas moins de leur humeur que de la fortune.*
The happiness and the unhappiness of men depends on their humors no less than on fortune.

62 *La sincérité est une ouverture de cœur. On la trouve en fort peu de gens; et celle que l'on voit d'ordinaire n'est qu'une fine dissimulation pour attirer la confiance des autres.*
Sincerity is an openness of the heart. One finds it in very few people; and what one ordinarily sees is only a subtle dissimulation in order to win the trust of others.

63 *L'aversion du mensonge est souvent une imperceptible ambition de ren-*

dre nos témoignages considérables, et d'attirer à nos paroles un respect de religion.

The aversion to lying is often an imperceptible ambition to render our statements weighty, and to win for our words the respect of religion.

64 *La vérité ne fait pas tant de bien dans le monde que ses apparences y font de mal.*

Truth does not cause as much good in the world as the appearance of it causes evil.

65 *Il n'y a point d'éloges qu'on ne donne à la prudence. Cependant elle ne saurait nous assurer du moindre événement.*

There is no praise which is not granted to prudence. Yet it could not assure us of the least of events.

66 *Un habile homme doit régler le rang de ses intérêts et les conduire chacun dans son ordre. Notre avidité le trouble souvent en nous faisant courir à tant de choses à la fois que, pour désirer trop les moins importantes, on manque les plus considérables.*

A clever man has to regulate the ranking of his interests and guide each of them in order. Our greed often troubles it by making us run after so many things at once that, by desiring the least important ones too much, we fail to obtain the more weighty.

67 *La bonne grâce est au corps ce que le bon sens est à l'esprit.*

Good grace is to the body what good sense is to the mind.

68 *Il est difficile de définir l'amour. Ce qu'on en peut dire est que dans l'âme c'est une passion de régner, dans les esprits c'est une sympathie, et dans le corps ce n'est qu'une envie cachée et délicate de posséder ce que l'on aime après beaucoup de mystères.*

68 It is difficult to define love. One can say that in the soul it is a passion to rule; in the mind, it is a sympathy; and in the body, it is only a hidden and delicate desire to possess what one loves after many mysteries.

69 *S'il y a un amour pur et exempt du mélange de nos autres passions, c'est celui qui est caché au fond du cœur, et que nous ignorons nous-mêmes.*
If there is a love pure and exempt from the *mélange* of our other passions, it is the one hidden at the bottom of our hearts, and of which we ourselves are unaware.

70 *Il n'y a point de déguisement qui puisse longtemps cacher l'amour où il est, ni le feindre où il n'est pas.*
There is no disguise that can for long hide love where it is, or feign it where it is not.

71 *Il n'y a guère de gens qui ne soient honteux de s'être aimés quand ils ne s'aiment plus.*
There are few people who are not ashamed to have loved each other once they no longer love each other.

72 *Si on juge de l'amour par la plupart de ses effets, il ressemble plus à la haine qu'à l'amitié.*
If one judges love by most of its effects, it resembles hatred more than friendship.

73 *On peut trouver des femmes qui n'ont jamais eu de galanterie; mais il est rare d'en trouver qui n'en aient jamais eu qu'une.*
One can find women who have never had any love affairs; but it is rare to find a woman who has had only one.

74 *Il n'y a que d'une sorte d'amour, mais il y en a mille différentes copies.*

74 There is only one kind of love, but there are a thousand different imitations.

75 *L'amour aussi bien que le feu ne peut subsister sans un mouvement continuel; et il cesse de vivre dès qu'il cesse d'espérer ou de craindre.*
Love as well as fire cannot subsist without continual movement; and it ceases to live as soon as it ceases to hope or to fear.

76 *Il est du véritable amour comme de l'apparition des esprits: tout le monde en parle, mais peu de gens en ont vu.*
True love is like an apparition of spirits: everyone talks about them, but few people have seen one.

77 *L'amour prête son nom à un nombre infini de commerces qu'on lui attribue, et où il n'a non plus de part que le Doge à ce qui se fait à Venise.*
Love lends its name to an infinite number of relations that are attributed to it, and in which love has no greater part than the Doge has in what is done in Venice.

78 *L'amour de la justice n'est en la plupart des hommes que la crainte de souffrir l'injustice.*
The love of justice is in most men only the fear of suffering injustice.

79 *Le silence est le parti le plus sûr de celui qui se défie de soi-même.*
Silence is the surest choice for someone diffident about himself.

80 *Ce qui nous rend si changeants dans nos amitiés, c'est qu'il est difficile de connaître les qualités de l'âme, et facile de connaître celles de l'esprit.*
What makes us so fickle in our friendships is that it is difficult to know the qualities of the soul, and easy to know those of the mind.

81 *Nous ne pouvons rien aimer que par rapport à nous, et nous ne faisons que suivre notre goût et notre plaisir quand nous préférons nos amis à nous-mêmes; c'est néanmoins par cette préférence seule que l'amitié peut être vraie et parfaite.*

We can love nothing but in relation to ourselves, and we are only following our taste and our pleasure when we prefer our friends to ourselves. It is nevertheless by this preference alone that friendship can be true and perfect.

82 *La réconciliation avec nos ennemis n'est qu'un désir de rendre notre condition meilleure, une lassitude de la guerre, et une crainte de quelque mauvais événement.*

Reconciliation with our enemies is only a desire to make our condition better, a weariness of war, and a fear of some bad event.

83 *Ce que les hommes ont nommé amitié n'est qu'une société, qu'un ménagement réciproque d'intérêts et qu'un échange de bons offices; ce n'est enfin qu'un commerce où l'amour-propre se propose toujours quelque chose à gagner.*

What men have named friendship is only a society, only a reciprocal management of interests, and only an exchange of good offices; it is, finally, only a relation in which self-love always presents itself with something to gain.

84 *Il est plus honteux de se défier de ses amis que d'en être trompé.*

It is more shameful to distrust one's friends than to be deceived by them.

85 *Nous nous persuadons souvent d'aimer les gens plus puissants que nous; et néanmoins c'est l'intérêt seul qui produit notre amitié. Nous ne nous donnons pas à eux pour le bien que nous leur voulons faire, mais pour celui que nous en voulons recevoir.*

85 We often persuade ourselves to love people more powerful than ourselves; and nevertheless, it is self-interest alone which produces our friendship. We do not give ourselves to them for the good we want to do to them, but for the good we want to receive from them.

86 *Notre défiance justifie la tromperie d'autrui.*
Our distrust justifies the deception of others.

87 *Les hommes ne vivraient pas longtemps en société s'ils n'étaient les dupes les uns des autres.*
Men would not live long in society if they were not one another's dupes.

88 *L'amour-propre nous augmente ou nous diminue les bonnes qualités de nos amis à proportion de la satisfaction que nous avons d'eux; et nous jugeons de leur mérite par la manière dont ils vivent avec nous.*
Self-love increases or decreases the good qualities of our friends to us in proportion to the satisfaction we receive from them; and we judge their merit by the manner in which they get on with us.

89 *Tout le monde se plaint de sa mémoire, et personne ne se plaint de son jugement.*
Everybody complains of his memory, and nobody complains of his judgment.

90 *Nous plaisons plus souvent dans le commerce de la vie par nos défauts que par nos bonnes qualités.*
We please more often in the commerce of life by our shortcomings than by our good qualities.

91 *La plus grande ambition n'en a pas la moindre apparence lorsqu'elle se rencontre dans une impossibilité absolue d'arriver où elle aspire.*

91 The greatest ambition does not in the least appear when it faces an absolute impossibility of attaining that to which it aspires.

92 *Détromper un homme préoccupé de son mérite est lui rendre un aussi mauvais office que celui que l'on rendit à ce fou d'Athènes, qui croyait que tous les vaisseaux qui arrivaient dans le port étaient à lui.*
Disillusioning a man preoccupied with his own merit is doing him as bad a turn as was done to that fool from Athens who believed that all the ships arriving in the port were his.[1]

93 *Les vieillards aiment à donner de bons préceptes, pour se consoler de n'être plus en état de donner de mauvais exemples.*
Old people enjoy giving good precepts to console themselves for not being in a position anymore to set bad examples.

94 *Les grands noms abaissent, au lieu d'élever, ceux qui ne les savent pas soutenir.*
Great names debase, instead of elevating, those who cannot uphold them.

95 *La marque d'un mérite extraordinaire est de voir que ceux qui l'envient le plus sont contraints de le louer.*
The mark of an extraordinary merit is to see those who envy it most are constrained to praise it.

96 *Tel homme est ingrat, qui est moins coupable de son ingratitude que celui qui lui a fait du bien.*
Such a man is ungrateful, who is less guilty of his ungratefulness, than the one who has done him good.

---

1 La Rochefoucauld is alluding to Thrasylles, who regretted losing his madness once he had been cured of it. This story is found in Athenaeus's *The Deipnosophists*, XII, 554.

97 *On s'est trompé lorsqu'on a cru que l'esprit et le jugement étaient deux choses différentes. Le jugement n'est que la grandeur de la lumière de l'esprit; cette lumière pénètre le fond des choses; elle y remarque tout ce qu'il faut remarquer et aperçoit celles qui semblent imperceptibles. Ainsi il faut demeurer d'accord que c'est l'étendue de la lumière de l'esprit qui produit tous les effets qu'on attribue au jugement.*

One was mistaken when one believed that the mind and the judgment were two different things. Judgment is only the greatness of the enlightenment of the mind; this enlightenment penetrates to the bottom of things; it notices there all that has to be noticed, and it perceives those things which seem imperceptible. Thus, it is necessary to agree that it is the extent of the enlightenment of the mind which produces all of the effects one attributes to judgment.

98 *Chacun dit du bien de son cœur, et personne n'en ose dire de son esprit.*
Everybody speaks well of his heart, and nobody dares to speak well of his mind.

99 *La politesse de l'esprit consiste à penser des choses honnêtes et délicates.*
The politeness of the mind consists in thinking of honest and delicate things.

100 *La galanterie de l'esprit est de dire des choses flatteuses d'une manière agréable.*
The gallantry of the mind is saying flattering things in an agreeable manner.

101 *Il arrive souvent que des choses se présentent plus achevées à notre esprit qu'il ne les pourrait faire avec beaucoup d'art.*
It often happens that some things present themselves as more accomplished to our mind than the mind could make them with much artfulness.

102 *L'esprit est toujours la dupe du cœur.*
The mind is always the dupe of the heart.

103 *Tous ceux qui connaissent leur esprit ne connaissent pas leur cœur.*
Not all those who know their mind know their heart.[2]

104 *Les hommes et les affaires ont leur point de perspective. Il y en a qu'il faut voir de près pour en bien juger, et d'autres dont on ne juge jamais si bien que quand on en est éloigné.*
Men and affairs have their point of perspective. Some must be seen close up to judge them well, and one never judges others so well as when one is far from them.

105 *Celui-là n'est pas raisonnable à qui le hasard fait trouver la raison, mais celui qui la connaît, qui la discerne, et qui la goûte.*
He is not reasonable to whom chance revealed reason, but he who knows it, who discerns it, and who savours it, is reasonable.

106 *Pour bien savoir les choses, il en faut savoir le détail; et comme il est presque infini, nos connaissances sont toujours superficielles et imparfaites.*
Knowing things well requires knowing the details; and as they are almost infinite, our knowledge is always superficial and imperfect.

107 *C'est une espèce de coquetterie de faire remarquer qu'on n'en fait jamais.*
It is a kind of coquetry to point out that one is never coquettish.

108 *L'esprit ne saurait jouer longtemps le personnage du cœur.*
The mind cannot for long play the role of the heart.

2   This maxim admits of another translation: "All those who know their mind do not know their heart."

109 *La jeunesse change ses goûts par l'ardeur du sang, et la vieillesse conserve les siens par l'accoutumance.*
Youth changes its tastes by the ardor of the blood, and old age conserves them by habit.

110 *On ne donne rien si libéralement que ses conseils.*
One gives nothing so liberally as pieces of advice.

111 *Plus on aime une maîtresse, et plus on est près de la haïr.*
The more one loves a mistress, the closer one is to hating her.

112 *Les défauts de l'esprit augmentent en vieillissant comme ceux du visage.*
The shortcomings of the mind increase with age like those of the face.

113 *Il y a de bons mariages, mais il n'y en a point de délicieux.*
There are good marriages, but none is delicious.

114 *On ne se peut consoler d'être trompé par ses ennemis, et trahi par ses amis; et l'on est souvent satisfait de l'être par soi-même.*
One cannot console oneself for being deceived by one's enemies, and betrayed by one's friends; and one is often satisfied to be deceived and betrayed by oneself.

115 *Il est aussi facile de se tromper soi-même sans s'en apercevoir qu'il est difficile de tromper les autres sans qu'ils s'en aperçoivent.*
It is as easy to deceive oneself without noticing it as it is difficult to deceive others without their noticing it.

116 *Rien n'est moins sincère que la manière de demander et de donner des conseils. Celui qui en demande paraît avoir une déférence respectueuse pour les sentiments de son ami, bien qu'il ne pense qu'à lui faire*

*approuver les siens, et à le rendre garant de sa conduite. Et celui qui
conseille paye la confiance qu'on lui témoigne d'un zèle ardent et désintéressé, quoiqu'il ne cherche le plus souvent dans les conseils qu'il
donne que son propre intérêt ou sa gloire.*

Nothing is less sincere than the manner of seeking and giving
advice. He who seeks advice seems to have a respectful deference for the sentiments of his friend, whereas he only thinks of
making him approve his own, and to make his friend answer for
his conduct. And he who advises repays the confidence he is
shown with an ardent and disinterested zeal, even though most
often he only seeks in the advice he gives his own self-interest
or glory.

117 *La plus subtile de toutes les finesses est de savoir bien feindre de tomber
dans les pièges que l'on nous tend, et on n'est jamais si aisément trompé
que quand on songe à tromper les autres.*

The most subtle of all shrewdness is knowing well how to feign
falling into the snares that are set for us, and one is never so easily deceived as when one intends to deceive others.

118 *L'intention de ne jamais tromper nous expose à être souvent trompés.*

The intention of never deceiving exposes us to being often
deceived.

119 *Nous sommes si accoutumés à nous déguiser aux autres qu'enfin nous
nous déguisons à nous-mêmes.*

We are so accustomed to disguise ourselves from others that we
end up disguising ourselves from ourselves.

120 *L'on fait plus souvent des trahisons par faiblesse que par un dessein
formé de trahir.*

One commits treason more often from weakness than from a
design to betray.

121 *On fait souvent du bien pour pouvoir impunément faire du mal.*
One often does good in order to be able to do evil with impunity.

122 *Si nous résistons à nos passions, c'est plus par leur faiblesse que par notre force.*
If we resist our passions, it is more through their weakness than through our strength.

123 *On n'aurait guère de plaisir si on ne se flattait jamais.*
One would hardly have any pleasure if one never flattered oneself.

124 *Les plus habiles affectent toute leur vie de blâmer les finesses pour s'en servir en quelque grande occasion et pour quelque grand intérêt.*
The most clever pretend all their lives to blame shrewdness in order to use it on some great occasion and for some great interest.

125 *L'usage ordinaire de la finesse est la marque d'un petit esprit, et il arrive presque toujours que celui qui s'en sert pour se couvrir en un endroit, se découvre en un autre.*
The ordinary usage of shrewdness is the mark of a small mind; and it happens almost always that he who uses it to cover himself in one place, uncovers himself in another.

126 *Les finesses et les trahisons ne viennent que de manque d'habileté.*
Shrewdness and betrayal come only from a lack of cleverness.

127 *Le vrai moyen d'être trompé, c'est de se croire plus fin que les autres.*
The true means of being deceived is to believe oneself shrewder than others.

128 La trop grande subtilité est une fausse délicatesse; et la véritable délicatesse est une solide subtilité.
Too great a subtlety is a false refinement; and true refinement is a sound subtlety.

129 Il suffit quelquefois d'être grossier pour n'être pas trompé par un habile homme.
It is sometimes sufficient to be rude in order not to be deceived by a clever man.

130 La faiblesse est le seul défaut que l'on ne saurait corriger.
Weakness is the only shortcoming one cannot correct.

131 Le moindre défaut des femmes qui se sont abandonnées à faire l'amour, c'est de faire l'amour.
The least shortcoming of women who have abandoned themselves to making love is making love.

132 Il est plus aisé d'être sage pour les autres que de l'être pour soi-même.
It is easier to be wise for others than for oneself.

133 Les seules bonnes copies sont celles qui nous font voir le ridicule des méchants originaux.
The only good copies are those that make us see the ridiculousness of bad originals.

134 On n'est jamais si ridicule par les qualités que l'on a que par celles que l'on affecte d'avoir.
One is never so ridiculous through the qualities one has as through those one pretends to have.

135 On est quelquefois aussi différent de soi-même que des autres.

135 One is sometimes as different from oneself as from others.

136 *Il y a des gens qui n'auraient jamais été amoureux s'ils n'avaient jamais entendu parler de l'amour.*
There are people who would never have been in love if they had never heard about love.

137 *On parle peu quand la vanité ne fait pas parler.*
One speaks little when vanity does not make one speak.

138 *On aime mieux dire du mal de soi-même que de n'en point parler.*
One prefers to speak ill of oneself than not to speak of oneself.

139 *Une des choses qui fait que l'on trouve si peu de gens qui paraissent raisonnables et agréables dans la conversation, c'est qu'il n'y a presque personne qui ne pense plutôt à ce qu'il veut dire qu'à répondre précisément à ce qu'on lui dit. Les plus habiles et les plus complaisants se contentent de montrer seulement une mine attentive, au même temps que l'on voit dans leurs yeux et dans leur esprit un égarement pour ce qu'on leur dit, et une précipitation pour retourner à ce qu'ils veulent dire; au lieu de considérer que c'est un mauvais moyen de plaire aux autres ou de les persuader, que de chercher si fort à se plaire à soi-même, et que bien écouter et bien répondre est une des plus grandes perfections qu'on puisse avoir dans la conversation.*
One of the things that leads one to find so few people who seem reasonable and agreeable in conversation is that there is almost nobody who does not think rather about what he wants to say than responding precisely to what is said to him. The most clever and the most complaisant are content only to show an attentive countenance, while at the same time, one sees in their eyes and in their mind a bewilderment at what is said to them, and a hastiness to return to what they want to say, instead of

considering that seeking so hard to please oneself is a bad means of pleasing others or persuading them, and that listening well and responding well is one of the greatest perfections that one can have in conversation.

140 *Un homme d'esprit serait souvent bien embarrassé sans la compagnie des sots.*

A man of wit would often be very embarrassed without the company of idiots.

141 *Nous nous vantons souvent de ne nous point ennuyer; et nous sommes si glorieux que nous ne voulons pas nous trouver de mauvaise compagnie.*

We often boast that we are never bored; and we are so vainglorious that we do not want to find our own company bad.

142 *Comme c'est le caractère des grands esprits de faire entendre en peu de paroles beaucoup de choses, les petits esprits au contraire ont le don de beaucoup parler, et de ne rien dire.*

As it is the character of great minds to make many things understood with few words, so small minds, to the contrary, have the gift of talking a lot and of saying nothing.

143 *C'est plutôt par l'estime de nos propres sentiments que nous exagérons les bonnes qualités des autres, que par l'estime de leur mérite; et nous voulons nous attirer des louanges, lorsqu'il semble que nous leur en donnons.*

It is rather from the esteem for our own sentiments that we exaggerate the good qualities of others, than from the esteem of their merit; and we want to win praise for ourselves while seeming to praise them.

144 *On n'aime point à louer, et on ne loue jamais personne sans intérêt. La*

louange est une flatterie habile, cachée, et délicate, qui satisfait dif-féremment celui qui la donne, et celui qui la reçoit. L'un la prend comme une récompense de son mérite; l'autre la donne pour faire remarquer son équité et son discernement.

One does not like to praise, and one never praises anyone without self-interest. Praise is a clever flattery, hidden, and delicate, that satisfies differently he who gives it, and he who receives it. One takes it as a reward for his merit; the other gives it to call attention to his equity and his discernment.

145 *Nous choisissons souvent des louanges empoisonnées qui font voir par contrecoup en ceux que nous louons des défauts que nous n'osons décou-vrir d'une autre sorte.*

We often choose venomous praise which indirectly reveals some shortcomings in those we praise that we do not dare unveil in another way.

146 *On ne loue d'ordinaire que pour être loué.*

One ordinarily praises only to be praised.

147 *Peu de gens sont assez sages pour préférer le blâme qui leur est utile à la louange qui les trahit.*

Few people are wise enough to prefer the blame that is useful to them to the praise that betrays them.

148 *Il y a des reproches qui louent, et des louanges qui médisent.*

There are reproaches that praise, and praises that slander.

149 *Le refus des louanges est un désir d'être loué deux fois.*

The refusal of praise is a desire to be praised twice.

150 *Le désir de mériter les louanges qu'on nous donne fortifie notre vertu; et celles que l'on donne à l'esprit, à la valeur, et à la beauté contribuent à les augmenter.*

150 The desire to merit the praises that we are given fortifies our virtue; and the praises that we give to the mind, to valor, and to beauty contribute to increasing them.

151 *Il est plus difficile de s'empêcher d'être gouverné que de gouverner les autres.*
It is more difficult to restrain oneself from being governed than to govern others.

152 *Si nous ne nous flattions point nous-mêmes, la flatterie des autres ne nous pourrait nuire.*
If we did not flatter ourselves, the flattery of others could not harm us.

153 *La nature fait le mérite, et la fortune le met en œuvre.*
Nature makes merit, and fortune puts it to work.

154 *La fortune nous corrige de plusieurs défauts que la raison ne saurait corriger.*
Fortune corrects several of our shortcomings that reason cannot correct.

155 *Il y a des gens dégoûtants avec du mérite, et d'autres qui plaisent avec des défauts.*
There are some disgusting people with merit, and others who please with shortcomings.

156 *Il y a des gens dont tout le mérite consiste à dire et à faire des sottises utilement, et qui gâteraient tout s'ils changeaient de conduite.*
There are people whose entire merit consists in saying and doing idiotic things usefully, and who would spoil everything if they changed their conduct.

157 *La gloire des grands hommes se doit toujours mesurer aux moyens dont ils se sont servis pour l'acquérir.*

The glory of great men must always be measured against the means they used to acquire it.

158 *La flatterie est une fausse monnaie qui n'a de cours que par notre vanité.*

Flattery is a counterfeit money given currency only by our vanity.

159 *Ce n'est pas assez d'avoir de grandes qualités; il en faut avoir l'économie.*

It is not enough to have great qualities; they must be used with economy.

160 *Quelque éclatante que soit une action, elle ne doit pas passer pour grande lorsqu'elle n'est pas l'effet d'un grand dessein.*

However dazzling an action may be, it should not pass for great when it is not the result of a great design.

161 *Il doit y avoir une certaine proportion entre les actions et les desseins si on en veut tirer tous les effets qu'elles peuvent produire.*

There has to be a certain proportion between actions and designs if one wants to derive from these actions all of the results they can produce.

162 *L'art de savoir bien mettre en œuvre de médiocres qualités dérobe l'estime et donne souvent plus de réputation que le véritable mérite.*

The art of knowing well how to bring mediocre qualities into play defrauds esteem and often gives more reputation than true merit.

163 *Il y a une infinité de conduites qui paraissent ridicules, et dont les raisons cachées sont très sages et très solides.*

There are infinite courses of conduct that appear ridiculous, and whose hidden reasons are very wise and very solid.

164 *Il est plus facile de paraître digne des emplois qu'on n'a pas que de ceux que l'on exerce.*

It is easier to appear worthy of the occupations one does not have than of those one practices.

165 *Notre mérite nous attire l'estime des honnêtes gens, et notre étoile celle du public.*

Our merit wins us the esteem of honorable people, and our lucky stars that of the public.

166 *Le monde récompense plus souvent les apparences du mérite que le mérite même.*

The world more often rewards the appearance of merit than merit itself.

167 *L'avarice est plus opposée à l'économie que la libéralité.*

Avarice is more opposed to economy than liberality.

168 *L'espérance, toute trompeuse qu'elle est, sert au moins à nous mener à la fin de la vie par un chemin agréable.*

Hope, however deceiving it is, is at least useful for leading one to the end of life along an agreeable road.

169 *Pendant que la paresse et la timidité nous retiennent dans notre devoir, notre vertu en a souvent tout l'honneur.*

While laziness and timidity keep us to our duty, our virtue often receives all the honor for it.

170 Il est difficile de juger si un procédé net, sincère et honnête est un effet de probité ou d'habileté

It is difficult to judge whether a straightforward, sincere, and honest proceeding is a result of probity or cleverness.

171 Les vertus se perdent dans l'intérêt, comme les fleuves se perdent dans la mer.

Virtues lose themselves in self-interest, as rivers lose themselves in the sea.

172 Si on examine bien les divers effets de l'ennui, on trouvera qu'il fait manquer à plus de devoirs que l'intérêt.

If one examines well the various effects of *ennui*, one will find that it makes one neglect more duties than self-interest does.

173 Il y a diverses sortes de curiosité: l'une d'intérêt, qui nous porte à désirer d'apprendre ce qui nous peut être utile, et l'autre d'orgueil, qui vient du désir de savoir ce que les autres ignorent.

There are various sorts of curiosity: the one from self-interest, which induces us to desire to learn what can be useful to us; and the other from pride, which comes from the desire to know what others ignore.

174 Il vaut mieux employer notre esprit à supporter les infortunes qui nous arrivent qu'à prévoir celles qui nous peuvent arriver.

It is better to employ our minds to bear the misfortunes which happen to us rather than foreseeing those which can happen to us.

175 La constance en amour est une inconstance perpétuelle, qui fait que notre cœur s'attache successivement à toutes les qualités de la personne que nous aimons, donnant tantôt la préférence à l'une, tantôt à l'autre;

*de sorte que cette constance n'est qu'une inconstance arrêtée et renfer-
mée dans un même sujet.*

Constancy in love is a perpetual inconstancy, which makes our
heart bind itself in succession to all the qualities of the person
we love, now giving the preference to one, now to the other; so
that this constancy is merely an inconstancy fixed and confined
to one subject only.

176 *Il y a deux sortes de constance en amour: l'une vient de ce que l'on
trouve sans cesse dans la personne que l'on aime de nouveaux sujets
d'aimer, et l'autre vient de ce que l'on se fait un honneur d'être constant.*

There are two sorts of constancy in love: the one comes from the
fact that one unceasingly finds in the person one loves new reasons to love; and the other comes from the fact that one glories
in being constant.

177 *La persévérance n'est digne ni de blâme ni de louange, parce qu'elle
n'est que la durée des goûts et des sentiments, qu'on ne s'ôte et qu'on ne
se donne point.*

Perseverance is worthy neither of blame nor of praise, because
it is only the duration of tastes and sentiments, which one neither takes away from, nor gives to oneself.

178 *Ce qui nous fait aimer les nouvelles connaissances n'est pas tant la lassitude que nous avons des vieilles ou le plaisir de changer, que le dégoût
de n'être pas assez admirés de ceux qui nous connaissent trop, et l'espérance de l'être davantage de ceux qui ne nous connaissent pas tant.*

What makes us like new acquaintances is not so much the
weariness we have of the old ones or the pleasure of changing,
as the disgust of not being admired enough by those who know
us too well, and the hope of being more admired by those who
do not know us as well.

179 Nous nous plaignons quelquefois légèrement de nos amis pour justifier par avance notre légèreté.

We sometimes complain lightly of our friends in order to justify in advance our own lightness.

180 Notre repentir n'est pas tant un regret du mal que nous avons fait, qu'une crainte de celui qui nous en peut arriver.

Our repentance is not so much a regret of the evil we have done, as a fear of what can befall us from it.

181 Il y a une inconstance qui vient de la légèreté de l'esprit ou de sa faiblesse, qui lui fait recevoir toutes les opinions d'autrui, et il y en a une autre, qui est plus excusable, qui vient du dégoût des choses.

There is an inconstancy which comes from the flightiness of mind, or from its weakness, which makes it receive all the opinions of others, and there is another one, which is more excusable, which comes from disgust with things.

182 Les vices entrent dans la composition des vertus comme les poisons entrent dans la composition des remèdes. La prudence les assemble et les tempère, et elle s'en sert utilement contre les maux de la vie.

Vices enter into the composition of virtues like poisons enter into the composition of remedies. Prudence assembles them and tempers them, and it uses them effectively against the ills of life.

183 Il faut demeurer d'accord à l'honneur de la vertu que les plus grands malheurs des hommes sont ceux où ils tombent par les crimes.

One has to agree, to the honor of virtue, that the greatest misfortunes of men are those into which they fall through crimes.

184 Nous avouons nos défauts pour réparer par notre sincérité le tort qu'ils nous font dans l'esprit des autres.

184 We confess our shortcomings to repair with our sincerity the harm these do us in the minds of others.

185 *Il y a des héros en mal comme en bien.*
There are heroes in evil as in good.

186 *On ne méprise pas tous ceux qui ont des vices; mais on méprise tous ceux qui n'ont aucune vertu.*
One does not have contempt for all those who have vices, but one has contempt for all those who have no virtue at all.

187 *Le nom de la vertu sert à l'intérêt aussi utilement que les vices.*
The name of virtue serves self-interest as usefully as vices.

188 *La santé de l'âme n'est pas plus assurée que celle du corps; et quoique l'on paraisse éloigné des passions, on n'est pas moins en danger de s'y laisser emporter que de tomber malade quand on se porte bien.*
The health of the soul is no more assured than that of the body; and although one appears distant from the passions, one is no less in danger of letting oneself be carried away by them than of falling ill when one is in good health.

189 *Il semble que la nature ait prescrit à chaque homme dès sa naissance des bornes pour les vertus et pour les vices.*
It seems that nature has prescribed to each man from his birth the limits for virtues and vices.

190 *Il n'appartient qu'aux grands hommes d'avoir de grands défauts.*
It is only for great men to have great shortcomings.

191 *On peut dire que les vices nous attendent dans le cours de la vie comme des hôtes chez qui il faut successivement loger; et je doute que l'expé-*

*rience nous les fit éviter s'il nous était permis de faire deux fois le
même chemin.*

One may say that vices wait for us in the course of life as hosts
with whom one has to be housed in succession; and I doubt that
experience would make us avoid them if we were permitted to
follow the same road twice.

192 *Quand les vices nous quittent, nous nous flattons de la créance que c'est
nous qui les quittons.*

When vices leave us, we flatter ourselves with the belief that it
is we who leave them.

193 *Il y a des rechutes dans les maladies de l'âme, comme dans celles du
corps. Ce que nous prenons pour notre guérison n'est le plus souvent
qu'un relâche ou un changement de mal.*

There are relapses in the illnesses of the soul like in those of the
body. What we take to be our cure is often only a respite or a
change of illness.

194 *Les défauts de l'âme sont comme les blessures du corps: quelque soin
qu'on prenne de les guérir, la cicatrice paraît toujours, et elles sont à
tout moment en danger de se rouvrir.*

The shortcomings of the soul are like the wounds of the body:
whatever care one takes to heal them, the scars are always visible, and they are at all moments in danger of reopening.

195 *Ce qui nous empêche souvent de nous abandonner à un seul vice est
que nous en avons plusieurs.*

What often prevents us from abandoning ourselves to only one
vice is that we have several.

196 *Nous oublions aisément nos fautes lorsqu'elles ne sont sues que de nous.*

196 We easily forget our faults when they are known only by our-selves.

197 *Il y a des gens de qui l'on peut ne jamais croire du mal sans l'avoir vu; mais il n'y en a point en qui il nous doive surprendre en le voy-ant.*

There are people of whom one can never expect evil without having seen it; but there is no one in whom it should surprise us when we see it.

198 *Nous élevons la gloire des uns pour abaisser celle des autres. Et quelquefois on louerait moins Monsieur le Prince et M. de Turenne si on ne les voulait point blâmer tous deux.*

We elevate the glory of some to debase that of others. And sometimes one would praise less Monsieur le Prince and M. de Turenne[3] if one did not want to blame them both.

199 *Le désir de paraître habile empêche souvent de le devenir.*

The desire to appear clever often prevents one from becoming so.

200 *La vertu n'irait pas si loin si la vanité ne lui tenait compagnie.*

Virtue would not go so far if vanity did not keep it company.

201 *Celui qui croit pouvoir trouver en soi-même de quoi se passer de tout le monde se trompe fort; mais celui qui croit qu'on ne peut se passer de lui se trompe encore davantage.*

He who believes he can find enough in himself so as to dispense

---

3   La Rochefoucauld is referring to the Prince de Condé (1621–1686) and to the Maréchal de Turenne (1611–1675). During the Fronde, which took place dur-ing the minority of Louis XIV, Condé, as general of the Frondeurs, lost sever-al battles to the Royal troops led by Turenne.

with everyone is very mistaken; but he who believes that he is indispensable to others is even more mistaken.

202 Les faux honnêtes gens sont ceux qui déguisent leurs défauts aux autres et à eux-mêmes. Les vrais honnêtes gens sont ceux qui les connaissent parfaitement et les confessent.
The false honorable people are those who disguise their shortcomings to others and to themselves. The true honorable people are those who know them perfectly and confess them.

203 Le vrai honnête homme est celui qui ne se pique de rien.
The true honorable man is he who never claims superiority over anything.

204 La sévérité des femmes est un ajustement et un fard qu'elles ajoutent à leur beauté.
The severity of women is an adornment and a make-up that they add to their beauty.

205 L'honnêteté des femmes est souvent l'amour de leur réputation et de leur repos.
The honesty of women is often the love of their reputation and tranquillity.

206 C'est être véritablement honnête homme que de vouloir être toujours exposé à la vue des honnêtes gens.
He is truly an honorable man who wants to be always exposed to the sight of honorable people.

207 La folie nous suit dans tous les temps de la vie. Si quelqu'un paraît sage, c'est seulement parce que ses folies sont proportionnées à son âge et à sa fortune.
Folly follows us at all times in life. If someone appears wise, it

is only because his follies are proportionate to his age and fortune.

*208 Il y a des gens niais qui se connaissent, et qui emploient habilement
leur niaiserie.*
There are silly people who know themselves, and who cleverly
employ their silliness.

209 Qui vit sans folie n'est pas si sage qu'il croit.
He who lives without folly is not as wise as he believes.

210 En vieillissant on devient plus fou, et plus sage.
With age one becomes more foolish, and more wise.

*211 Il y a des gens qui ressemblent aux vaudevilles, qu'on ne chante qu'un
certain temps.*
There are some people who resemble popular songs, which one
sings only for a certain time.

*212 La plupart des gens ne jugent des hommes que par la vogue qu'ils ont,
ou par leur fortune.*
Most people only judge of men from the vogue they have, or
from their fortune.

*213 L'amour de la gloire, la crainte de la honte, le dessein de faire fortune,
le désir de rendre notre vie commode et agréable, et l'envie d'abaisser
les autres, sont souvent les causes de cette valeur si célèbre parmi les
hommes.*
The love of glory, the fear of shame, the intention of making a
fortune, the desire to render our life commodious and agreeable, and the wish to debase others, are often the causes of that
valor so celebrated among men.

214 La valeur est dans les simples soldats un métier périlleux qu'ils ont pris pour gagner leur vie.

Valor is, for private soldiers, a perilous trade which they have undertaken in order to earn their living.

215 La parfaite valeur et la poltronnerie complète sont deux extrémités où l'on arrive rarement. L'espace qui est entre-deux est vaste, et contient toutes les autres espèces de courage: il n'y a pas moins de différence entre elles qu'entre les visages et les humeurs. Il y a des hommes qui s'exposent volontiers au commencement d'une action, et qui se relâchent et se rebutent aisément par sa durée. Il y en a qui sont contents quand ils ont satisfait à l'honneur du monde, et qui font fort peu de chose au-delà. On en voit qui ne sont pas toujours également maîtres de leur peur. D'autres se laissent quelquefois entraîner à des terreurs générales. D'autres vont à la charge parce qu'ils n'osent demeurer dans leurs postes. Il s'en trouve à qui l'habitude des moindres périls affermit le courage et les prépare à s'exposer à de plus grands. Il y en a qui sont braves à coups d'épée, et qui craignent les coups de mousquet; d'autres sont assures aux coups de mousquet, et appréhendent de se battre à coups d'épée. Tous ces courages de différentes espèces conviennent en ce que la nuit augmentant la crainte et cachant les bonnes et les mauvaises actions, elle donne la liberté de se ménager. Il y a encore un autre ménagement plus général; car on ne voit point d'homme qui fasse tout ce qu'il serait capable de faire dans une occasion s'il était assuré d'en revenir. De sorte qu'il est visible que la crainte de la mort ôte quelque chose de la valeur.

Perfect valor and complete cowardice are two extremes one rarely reaches. The space which is between the two is vast, and contains all the other kinds of courage: there is no less difference between them than between faces and humors. There are men who willingly expose themselves at the beginning of an action, and who slacken and are easily discouraged because of its duration. There are some who are content once they have satisfied the honor of the world, and do very few things beyond that. One sees some who are not always equally masters of their fear. Others let themselves be carried away by general terrors. Others charge because they do not dare to remain at their posts. There are some for whom the habit of facing lesser perils strengthens their courage and prepares them to expose themselves to greater ones. Some are brave fighting with swords, but fear fighting with muskets; others are confident fighting with muskets, and dread fighting with swords. All these different kinds of courage are suitable because, since night increases fear and hides good and bad actions, it gives one the liberty to act cautiously. There is still another more general caution: for one does not see a man do all he could on any occasion as he would if he were confident to come back from it. So that it is visible that the fear of death takes something away from valor.

216 *La parfaite valeur est de faire sans témoins ce qu'on serait capable de faire devant tout le monde.*
Perfect valor is doing without witnesses what one would be capable of doing in front of everybody.

217 *L'intrépidité est une force extraordinaire de l'âme qui l'élève au-dessus des troubles, des désordres et des émotions que la vue des grands périls pourrait exciter en elle; et c'est par cette force que les héros se maintiennent en un état paisible, et conservent l'usage libre de leur raison dans les accidents les plus surprenants et les plus terribles.*
Intrepidity is an extraodinary strength of the soul which elevates it above the troubles, disorders, and emotions that the sight of great perils could excite in it; and it is by this strength that heroes maintain themselves in a peaceful state, and preserve the free use of their reason in the most surprising and most terrible accidents.

218 L'hypocrisie est un hommage que le vice rend à la vertu.
Hypocrisy is an homage vice pays to virtue.

219 La plupart des hommes s'exposent assez dans la guerre pour sauver leur honneur. Mais peu se veulent toujours exposer autant qu'il est nécessaire pour faire réussir le dessein pour lequel ils s'exposent.
Most men expose themselves enough in war to save their honor; but few always want to expose themselves as much as is necessary to make the design for which they expose themselves succeed.

220 La vanité, la honte, et surtout le tempérament, font souvent la valeur des hommes, et la vertu des femmes.
Vanity, shame, and above all temperament, often produce the valor of men, and the virtue of women.

221 On ne veut point perdre la vie, et on veut acquérir de la gloire; ce qui fait que les braves ont plus d'adresse et d'esprit pour éviter la mort que les gens de chicane n'en ont pour conserver leur bien.
One does not want to lose one's life, and one wants to acquire glory; this makes the brave more skillful and spirited in avoiding death than quibblers have in preserving their goods.

222 Il n'y a guère de personnes qui dans le premier penchant de l'âge ne fassent connaître par où leur corps et leur esprit doivent défaillir.
There is hardly anyone who at the first sign of age does not reveal where his body and his mind are bound to fail.

223 Il est de la reconnaissance comme de la bonne foi des marchands: elle entretient le commerce; et nous ne payons pas parce qu'il est juste de nous acquitter, mais pour trouver plus facilement des gens qui nous prêtent.
The same is true of gratitude as of the good faith of merchants:

it supports commerce; and we do not pay because it is just to pay our debts, but in order to find people more easily to lend to us.

224 *Tous ceux qui s'acquittent des devoirs de la reconnaissance ne peuvent pas pour cela se flatter d'être reconnaissants.*
All those who fulfill the duties of gratitude cannot for this reason flatter themselves for being grateful.

225 *Ce qui fait le mécompte dans la reconnaissance qu'on attend des grâces que l'on a faites, c'est que l'orgueil de celui qui donne, et l'orgueil de celui qui reçoit, ne peuvent convenir du prix du bienfait.*
What causes disappointment in the gratitude we expect for the favors we have granted, is that the pride of him who gives, and the pride of him who receives, cannot agree upon the price of the benefaction.

226 *Le trop grand empressement qu'on a de s'acquitter d'une obligation est une espèce d'ingratitude.*
Too great an alacrity in discharging oneself of an obligation is a kind of ingratitude.

227 *Les gens heureux ne se corrigent guère; ils croient toujours avoir raison quand la fortune soutient leur mauvaise conduite.*
Happy people hardly mend their ways; they always believe they are right when fortune supports their bad conduct.

228 *L'orgueil ne veut pas devoir, et l'amour-propre ne veut pas payer.*
Pride does not want to owe, and self-love does not want to pay.

229 *Le bien que nous avons reçu de quelqu'un veut que nous respections le mal qu'il nous fait.*

229 The good we have received from someone requires that we respect the ill he does to us.

230 Rien n'est si contagieux que l'exemple, et nous ne faisons jamais de grands biens ni de grands maux qui n'en produisent de semblables. Nous imitons les bonnes actions par émulation, et les mauvaises par la malignité de notre nature que la honte retenait prisonnière, et que l'exemple met en liberté.

Nothing is so contagious as an example, and we never do any great good or any great evil which do not produce similar ones. We imitate the good actions through emulation, and the bad ones through the malignity of our nature that shame kept prisoner, and that an example sets free.

231 C'est une grande folie de vouloir être sage tout seul.

It is a great folly to want to be wise all alone.

232 Quelque prétexte que nous donnions à nos afflictions, ce n'est souvent que l'intérêt et la vanité qui les causent.

Whatever pretext we give to our afflictions, often it is only self-interest and vanity that cause them.

233 Il y a dans les afflictions diverses sortes d'hypocrisie. Dans l'une, sous prétexte de pleurer la perte d'une personne qui nous est chère, nous nous pleurons nous-mêmes; nous regrettons la bonne opinion qu'il[4] avait de nous; nous pleurons la diminution de notre bien, de notre plaisir, de notre considération. Ainsi les morts ont l'honneur des larmes

---

4   The masculine pronoun La Rochefoucauld uses here, which we render as "this person," is surprising. The general character of the maxim would make one expect the pronoun to be feminine in order to agree with the noun preceding it, namely, *personne*. It suggests that La Rochefoucald has a specific man in mind.

qui ne coulent que pour les vivants. Je dis que c'est une espèce d'hypocrisie, à cause que dans ces sortes d'afflictions on se trompe soi-même. Il y a une autre hypocrisie qui n'est pas si innocente, parce qu'elle impose à tout le monde: c'est l'affliction de certaines personnes qui aspirent à la gloire d'une belle et immortelle douleur. Après que le temps qui consume tout a fait cesser celle qu'elles avaient en effet, elles ne laissent pas d'opiniâtrer leurs pleurs, leurs plaintes, et leurs soupirs; elles prennent un personnage lugubre, et travaillent à persuader par toutes leurs actions que leur déplaisir ne finira qu'avec leur vie. Cette triste et fatigante vanité se trouve d'ordinaire dans les femmes ambitieuses. Comme leur sexe leur ferme tous les chemins qui mènent à la gloire, elles s'efforcent de se rendre célèbres par la montre d'une inconsolable affliction. Il y a encore une autre espèce de larmes qui n'ont que de petites sources qui coulent et se tarissent facilement: on pleure pour avoir la réputation d'être tendre, on pleure pour être plaint, on pleure pour être pleuré; enfin on pleure pour éviter la honte de ne pleurer pas.

There are in afflictions various sorts of hypocrisy. In one of them, under the pretext of weeping over the loss of a person who is dear to us, we weep over ourselves; we regret the good opinion this person had of us; we weep over the diminution of our goods, of our pleasure, of our esteem. Thus the dead have the honor of tears shed only for the living. I say that it is a kind of hypocrisy, because in these sorts of afflictions one deceives oneself. There is another hypocrisy that is not so innocent because it impresses everybody: it is the affliction of certain people who aspire to the glory of a beautiful and immortal sorrow. After time – which consumes everything – has made the affliction cease that they indeed had, they cannot refrain from their obstinate weepings, wailings, and sighs; they take on a lugubrious character and work to persuade with all their actions that their displeasure will end only with their life. This sad and tiring vanity is ordinarily found in ambitious women. Since their sex closes to them all the roads that lead to glory, they strive to make themselves famous by showing an inconsolable affliction. There is still another kind of tears that only have a small source and run and dry up easily. One weeps in order to have the reputation of being tender, one weeps in order to be pitied, one weeps in order to be weeped over; finally, one weeps in order to avoid the shame of not weeping.

234 C'est plus souvent par orgueil que par défaut de lumières qu'on s'oppose avec tant d'opiniâtreté aux opinions les plus suivies: on trouve les premières places prises dans le bon parti, et on ne veut point des dernières.

It is more often from pride than from lack of enlightenment that one opposes with so much obstinacy the most widely held opinions: one finds the first seats taken in the good party, and one does not want the last ones.

235 Nous nous consolons aisément des disgrâces de nos amis lorsqu'elles servent à signaler notre tendresse pour eux.

We easily console ourselves for the disgraces of our friends when these disgraces help signal our tenderness for them.

236 Il semble que l'amour-propre soit la dupe de la bonté, et qu'il s'oublie lui-même lorsque nous travaillons pour l'avantage des autres. Cependant c'est prendre le chemin le plus assuré pour arriver à ses fins; c'est prêter à usure sous prétexte de donner; c'est enfin s'acquérir tout le monde par un moyen subtil et délicat.

It seems that self-love is the dupe of goodness, and that it forgets itself when we work for the advantage of others. However, it is taking the safest road to achieve one's ends; it is lending in usury under the pretext of giving; finally, it is winning everybody over through a subtle and delicate means.

237 *Nul ne mérite d'être loué de bonté, s'il n'a pas la force d'être méchant: toute autre bonté n'est le plus souvent qu'une paresse ou une impuissance de la volonté.*

No one deserves to be praised for goodness if he does not have the strength to be mean; any other goodness is most often only a laziness or an impotence of the will.

238 *Il n'est pas si dangereux de faire du mal à la plupart des hommes que de leur faire trop de bien.*

It is not as dangerous to do ill to most men as to do them too much good.

239 *Rien ne flatte plus notre orgueil que la confiance des grands, parce que nous la regardons comme un effet de notre mérite, sans considérer qu'elle ne vient le plus souvent que de vanité, ou d'impuissance de garder le secret.*

Nothing flatters our pride more than the trust of the great, because we regard it as an effect of our merit, without considering that it most often comes from vanity, or from an inability to keep a secret.

240 *On peut dire de l'agrément séparé de la beauté que c'est une symétrie dont on ne sait point les règles, et un rapport secret des traits ensemble, et des traits avec les couleurs et avec l'air de la personne.*

One may say that pleasantness separated from beauty is a symmetry for which the rules are unknown, and a secret relation of the features to each other, and of the features to the colors and the bearing of the person.

241 *La coquetterie est le fond de l'humeur des femmes. Mais toutes ne la mettent pas en pratique, parce que la coquetterie de quelques-unes est retenue par la crainte ou par la raison.*

241 Coquetry is the foundation of the humors of women; but all do not put it into practice, because the coquetry of some of them is restrained by fear or by reason.

242 *On incommode souvent les autres quand on croit ne les pouvoir jamais incommoder.*
One often inconveniences others when one believes one can never inconvenience them.

243 *Il y a peu de choses impossibles d'elles-mêmes; et l'application pour les faire réussir nous manque plus que les moyens.*
There are few things impossible in and of themselves; and the application to make them succeed fails us more than the means.

244 *La souveraine habileté consiste à bien connaître le prix des choses.*
Sovereign cleverness consists in knowing well the price of things.

245 *C'est une grande habileté que de savoir cacher son habileté.*
It is a great cleverness to know how to hide one's cleverness.

246 *Ce qui paraît générosité n'est souvent qu'une ambition déguisée qui méprise de petits intérêts, pour aller à de plus grands.*
What appears as generosity is often only a disguised ambition which despises small matters of self-interest to seek greater ones.

247 *La fidélité qui paraît en la plupart des hommes n'est qu'une invention de l'amour-propre pour attirer la confiance. C'est un moyen de nous élever au-dessus des autres, et de nous rendre dépositaires des choses les plus importantes.*
The fidelity which appears in most men is only an invention of

self-love in order to win trust. It is a means of elevating our-selves above others, and of making ourselves trustees of the most important things.

248 *La magnanimité méprise tout pour avoir tout.*
Magnanimity despises everything in order to have everything.

249 *Il n'y a pas moins d'éloquence dans le ton de la voix, dans les yeux et dans l'air de la personne, que dans le choix des paroles.*
There is no less eloquence in the tone of voice, in the eyes, and in the bearing of the person, than in the choice of words.

250 *La véritable éloquence consiste à dire tout ce qu'il faut, et à ne dire que ce qu'il faut.*
True eloquence consists in saying everything necessary, and in saying only what is necessary.

251 *Il y a des personnes à qui les défauts siéent bien, et d'autres qui sont disgraciées avec leurs bonnes qualités.*
There are people whose shortcomings suit them well, and oth-ers who are disgraced by their good qualities.

252 *Il est aussi ordinaire de voir changer les goûts qu'il est extraordinaire de voir changer les inclinations.*
It is as ordinary to see tastes change as it is extraordinary to see inclinations change.

253 *L'intérêt met en œuvre toutes sortes de vertus et de vices.*
Self-interest sets to work all sorts of virtues and vices.

254 *L'humilité n'est souvent qu'une feinte soumission, dont on se sert pour soumettre les autres; c'est un artifice de l'orgueil qui s'abaisse pour*

s'élever; et bien qu'il se transforme en mille manières, il n'est jamais mieux déguisé et plus capable de tromper que lorsqu'il se cache sous la figure de l'humilité.

Humility is often only a feigned submission which one uses to subdue others; it is an artifice of pride which debases itself in order to elevate itself; and even though pride transforms itself in a thousand ways, it is never better disguised nor more capable of deceiving than when it hides itself under the figure of humility.

255 *Tous les sentiments ont chacun un ton de voix, des gestes et des mines qui leur sont propres. Et ce rapport bon ou mauvais, agréable ou désagréable, est ce qui fait que les personnes plaisent ou déplaisent.*

Every single sentiment has a tone of voice, gestures, and countenances distinctive to it. And whether the relations between them are good or bad, agreeable or disagreeable, makes people pleasing or displeasing.

256 *Dans toutes les professions chacun affecte une mine et un extérieur pour paraître ce qu'il veut qu'on le croie. Ainsi on peut dire que le monde n'est composé que de mines.*

In all professions everyone affects a countenance and an exterior in order to appear as he wants to be thought of. Thus one can say that the world is composed only of countenances.

257 *La gravité est un mystère du corps inventé pour cacher les défauts de l'esprit.*

Gravity is a mystery of the body invented to hide the shortcomings of the mind.

258 *Le bon goût vient plus du jugement que de l'esprit.*

Good taste comes more from judgment than from the mind.

259 *Le plaisir de l'amour est d'aimer; et l'on est plus heureux par la passion que l'on a que par celle que l'on donne.*

The pleasure of love is to love; and one is more happy from the passion one has than from the passion one gives.

260 *La civilité est un désir d'en recevoir, et d'être estimé poli.*

Civility is a desire to be treated civilly, and to be deemed polite.

261 *L'éducation que l'on donne d'ordinaire aux jeunes gens est un second amour-propre qu'on leur inspire.*

The education one ordinarily gives to young people is a second self-love with which one inspires them.

262 *Il n'y a point de passion où l'amour de soi-même règne si puissamment que dans l'amour; et on est toujours plus disposé à sacrifier le repos de ce qu'on aime qu'à perdre le sien.*

There is no passion in which the love of oneself rules so powerfully as in love; and one is always more disposed to sacrifice the rest of those whom one loves rather than to lose one's own.

263 *Ce qu'on nomme libéralité n'est le plus souvent que la vanité de donner, que nous aimons mieux que ce que nous donnons.*

What one calls liberality is most often only the vanity of giving, which we like better than that which we give.

264 *La pitié est souvent un sentiment de nos propres maux dans les maux d'autrui. C'est une habile prévoyance des malheurs où nous pouvons tomber; nous donnons du secours aux autres pour les engager à nous en donner en de semblables occasions; et ces services que nous leur rendons sont à proprement parler des biens que nous nous faisons à nous-mêmes par avance.*

Pity is often a sentiment of our own ills in the ills of others. It is a clever foresight of the misfortunes into which we can fall; we give succor to others in order to induce them to give us some on similar occasions; and these favors that we do for them are, properly speaking, goods we do to ourselves in advance.

265 *La petitesse de l'esprit fait l'opiniâtreté; et nous ne croyons pas aisément ce qui est au-delà de ce que nous voyons.*

Pettiness of the mind produces obstinacy; and we do not easily believe what is beyond what we see.

266 *C'est se tromper que de croire qu'il n'y ait que les violentes passions comme l'ambition et l'amour, qui puissent triompher des autres. La paresse, toute languissante qu'elle est, ne laisse pas d'en être souvent la maîtresse; elle usurpe sur tous les desseins et sur toutes les actions de la vie; elle y détruit et y consume insensiblement les passions et les vertus.*

One deceives oneself when one believes that only the violent passions such as ambition and love can triumph over the others. Laziness, however languishing it may be, is nevertheless often the master of them; it usurps all the designs and all the actions of life; it destroys and consumes insensibly the passions and virtues in life.

267 *La promptitude à croire le mal sans l'avoir assez examiné est un effet de l'orgueil et de la paresse. On veut trouver des coupables; et on ne veut pas se donner la peine d'examiner les crimes.*

Promptness to believe ill without having examined it enough is an effect of pride and laziness. One wants to find guilty ones; and one does not want to take the trouble of examining the crimes.

268 *Nous récusons des juges pour les plus petits intérêts, et nous voulons bien que notre réputation et notre gloire dépendent du jugement des hommes, qui nous sont tous contraires, ou par leur jalousie, ou par leur*

préoccupation, ou par leur peu de lumière; et ce n'est que pour les faire prononcer en notre faveur que nous exposons en tant de manières notre repos et notre vie.

We take exception to some judges for the slightest self-interest, and we accept that our reputation and our glory depend upon the judgment of men, who are all against us, either from their jealousy, or from their preoccupation, or from their lack of enlightenment; and it is only to have them declare themselves in our favor that we expose in so many ways our repose and our life.

269 *Il n'y a guère d'homme assez habile pour connaître tout le mal qu'il fait.*

There is hardly any man clever enough to know all the evil that he does.

270 *L'honneur acquis est caution de celui qu'on doit acquérir.*

Acquired honor is a pledge for the honor one has to acquire.

271 *La jeunesse est une ivresse continuelle: c'est la fièvre de la raison.*

Youth is a continual drunkenness: it is the fever of reason.

272 *Rien ne devrait plus humilier les hommes qui ont mérité de grandes louanges, que le soin qu'ils prennent encore de se faire valoir par de petites choses.*

Nothing should more humiliate the men who have deserved great praise than the care they still take to put themselves forward with small things.

273 *Il y a des gens qu'on approuve dans le monde, qui n'ont pour tout mérite que les vices qui servent au commerce de la vie.*

273 There are people who are approved of in society, and whose only merits are the vices that help the commerce of life.

274 *La grâce de la nouveauté est à l'amour ce que la fleur est sur les fruits; elle y donne un lustre qui s'efface aisément, et qui ne revient jamais.*
The grace of novelty is to love what the flower is over the fruits; it gives it luster which becomes easily erased, and which never comes back.

275 *Le bon naturel, qui se vante d'être si sensible, est souvent étouffé par le moindre intérêt.*
The good natured who boast about being so sensible are often choked by the smallest self-interest.

276 *L'absence diminue les médiocres passions, et augmente les grandes, comme le vent éteint les bougies et allume le feu.*
Absence diminishes the mediocre passions, and increases the great ones, like the wind extinguishes candles and fans the flames.

277 *Les femmes croient souvent aimer encore qu'elles n'aiment pas. L'occupation d'une intrigue, l'émotion d'esprit que donne la galanterie, la pente naturelle au plaisir d'être aimées, et la peine de refuser, leur persuadent qu'elles ont de la passion lorsqu'elles n'ont que de la coquetterie*
Women often believe they love though they do not. The pursuit of an intrigue, the emotion of the mind that a love affair gives, the natural bent toward the pleasure of being loved, and the pain of refusing, persuade them that they have passion when they have only coquetry.

278 *Ce qui fait que l'on est souvent mécontent de ceux qui négocient, est*

qu'ils abandonnent presque toujours l'intérêt de leurs amis pour l'in-
térêt du succès de la négociation, qui devient le leur par l'honneur
d'avoir réussi à ce qu'ils avaient entrepris.

What makes one often discontented with those who negotiate is
that they almost always abandon the interest of their friends for
the interest of the success of the negotiation, a success which
becomes theirs through the honor of having succeeded in what
they had undertaken.

279 *Quand nous exagérons la tendresse que nos amis ont pour nous, c'est*
souvent moins par reconnaissance que par le désir de faire juger de
notre mérite.

When we exaggerate the tenderness our friends have for us, it
is often less from gratitude than from the desire to have our
merit judged.

280 *L'approbation que l'on donne à ceux qui entrent dans le monde vient*
souvent de l'envie secrète que l'on porte à ceux qui y sont établis.

The approbation that one gives to those who enter into society
often comes from the secret envy one has for those who are
established in it.

281 *L'orgueil qui nous inspire tant d'envie nous sert souvent aussi à la*
modérer.

Pride, which inspires us with so much envy, also often helps us
moderate it.

282 *Il y a des faussetés déguisées qui représentent si bien la vérité que ce*
serait mal juger que de ne s'y pas laisser tromper.

There is a disguised duplicity which represents truth so well
that it would be to judge badly not to let oneself be deceived by
it.

283 *Il n'y a pas quelquefois moins d'habileté à savoir profiter d'un bon con-
seil qu'à se bien conseiller soi-même.*

Sometimes there is no less cleverness in knowing how to profit
from good advice than in advising oneself well.

284 *Il y a des méchants qui seraient moins dangereux s'ils n'avaient
aucune bonté.*

There are wicked people who would be less dangerous if they
had no goodness at all.

285 *La magnanimité est assez définie par son nom; néanmoins on pourrait
dire que c'est le bon sens de l'orgueil, et la voie la plus noble pour
recevoir des louanges.*

Magnanimity is tolerably defined by its name; nevertheless one
could say that it is the good sense of pride, and the noblest way
to receive praises.

286 *Il est impossible d'aimer une seconde fois ce qu'on a véritablement cessé
d'aimer.*

It is impossible to love a second time what one has truly ceased
to love.

287 *Ce n'est pas tant la fertilité de l'esprit qui nous fait trouver plusieurs
expédients sur une même affaire, que c'est le défaut de lumière qui nous
fait arrêter à tout ce qui se présente à notre imagination, et qui nous
empêche de discerner d'abord ce qui est le meilleur.*

It is not so much the fertility of the mind which makes us find
several contrivances for the same affair, as it is the lack of
enlightenment which makes us stop at everything that presents
itself to our imagination, and which prevents us from discern-
ing at first what is best.

288 *Il y a des affaires et des maladies que les remèdes aigrissent en certains temps; et la grande habileté consiste à connaître quand il est dangereux d'en user.*

There are affairs and illnesses that remedies sour at certain times; and great cleverness consists in knowing when it is dangerous to use them.

289 *La simplicité affectée est une imposture délicate.*

An affected simplicity is a delicate imposture.

290 *Il y a plus de défauts dans l'humeur que dans l'esprit.*

There are more shortcomings of humors than of the mind.

291 *Le mérite des hommes a sa saison aussi bien que les fruits.*

The merit of men has its season as well as fruits.

292 *On peut dire de l'humeur des hommes, comme de la plupart des bâtiments, qu'elle a diverses faces, les unes agréables, et les autres désagréables.*

One can say of the humors of men, as of most buildings, that they have various faces, some agreeable, and others disagreeable.

293 *La modération ne peut avoir le mérite de combattre l'ambition et de la soumettre: elles ne se trouvent jamais ensemble. La modération est la langueur et la paresse de l'âme, comme l'ambition en est l'activité et l'ardeur.*

Moderation cannot have the merit of fighting ambition and of subduing it: they are never found together. While moderation is the languor and laziness of the soul, ambition is its activity and ardor.

294 *Nous aimons toujours ceux qui nous admirent; et nous n'aimons pas toujours ceux que nous admirons.*

294 We always love those who admire us; and we do not always love those whom we admire.

295 *Il s'en faut bien que nous ne connaissions toutes nos volontés.*
We are very far from knowing all we want.

296 *Il est difficile d'aimer ceux que nous n'estimons point; mais il ne l'est pas moins d'aimer ceux que nous estimons beaucoup plus que nous.*
It is difficult to love those whom we do not esteem; but it is no less so to love those whom we esteem much more than ourselves.

297 *Les humeurs du corps ont un cours ordinaire et réglé, qui meut et qui tourne imperceptiblement notre volonté; elles roulent ensemble et exercent successivement un empire secret en nous: de sorte qu'elles ont une part considérable à toutes nos actions, sans que nous le puissions connaître.*
The humors of the body have an ordinary and regulated course, which imperceptibly move and turns our will; together they rule and exercise successively a secret dominion within us: so that they play a considerable part in all of our actions, without our being able to know it.

298 *La reconnaissance de la plupart des hommes n'est qu'une secrète envie de recevoir de plus grands bienfaits.*
The gratitude of most men is only a secret envy to receive greater benefactions.

299 *Presque tout le monde prend plaisir à s'acquitter des petites obligations; beaucoup de gens ont de la reconnaissance pour les médiocres; mais il n'y a quasi personne qui n'ait de l'ingratitude pour les grandes.*
Almost everybody takes pleasure in discharging small obligations; many people have gratitude for mediocre ones; but there is almost nobody who does not have ingratitude for great ones.

300 Il y a des folies qui se prennent comme les maladies contagieuses.
There are some follies which are caught like contagious diseases.

301 Assez de gens méprisent le bien, mais peu savent le donner.
Enough people despise wealth, but few know how to give it away.

302 Ce n'est d'ordinaire que dans de petits intérêts où nous prenons le hasard de ne pas croire aux apparences.
It is ordinarily only in minor matters that we take the chance of not believing in appearances.

303 Quelque bien qu'on nous dise de nous, on ne nous apprend rien de nouveau.
Whatever good we are told about ourselves, we are not taught anything new.

304 Nous pardonnons souvent à ceux qui nous ennuient, mais nous ne pouvons pardonner à ceux que nous ennuyons.
We often forgive those who bore us, but we cannot forgive those whom we bore.

305 L'intérêt que l'on accuse de tous nos crimes mérite souvent d'être loué de nos bonnes actions.
Self-interest which is accused of all of our crimes often deserves to be praised for our good actions.

306 On ne trouve guère d'ingrats tant qu'on est en état de faire du bien.
One hardly finds any ingrates as long as one is able to do some good.

307 Il est aussi honnête d'être glorieux avec soi-même qu'il est ridicule de l'être avec les autres.

307 It is as honest to be vainglorious with oneself as it is ridiculous to be so with others.

308 *On a fait une vertu de la modération pour borner l'ambition des grands hommes, et pour consoler les gens médiocres de leur peu de fortune, et de leur peu de mérite.*
People have made a virtue of moderation in order to limit the ambition of great men, and to console mediocre people for their limited fortune, and their limited merit.

309 *Il y a des gens destinés à être sots, qui ne font pas seulement des sottises par leur choix, mais que la fortune même contraint d'en faire.*
There are some people destined to be fools, who not only do foolish things by their own choice, but fortune herself constrains them to do some.

310 *Il arrive quelquefois des accidents dans la vie, d'où il faut être un peu fou pour se bien tirer.*
Sometimes accidents happen in life from which it is necessary to be a little crazy in order to escape.

311 *S'il y a des hommes dont le ridicule n'ait jamais paru, c'est qu'on ne l'a pas bien cherché.*
If there are men whose ridicule has never appeared, it is because one has not looked for it well enough.

312 *Ce qui fait que les amants et les maîtresses ne s'ennuient point d'être ensemble, c'est qu'ils parlent toujours d'eux-mêmes.*
The reason lovers and mistresses are not bored to be together is that they always speak of themselves.

313 *Pourquoi faut-il que nous ayons assez de mémoire pour retenir jusqu'aux moindres particularités de ce qui nous est arrivé, et que nous*

*n'en ayons pas assez pour nous souvenir combien de fois nous les avons
contées à une même personne?*

Why should we have enough memory to retain even the smallest details of what happened to us, while we do not have enough
to remember how many times we have told them to the same
person?

314 *L'extrême plaisir que nous prenons à parler de nous-mêmes nous doit
faire craindre de n'en donner guère à ceux qui nous écoutent.*

The extreme pleasure which we take in talking about ourselves
ought to make us fear that we hardly give any to those listening
to us.

315 *Ce qui nous empêche d'ordinaire de faire voir le fond de notre cœur à
nos amis, n'est pas tant la défiance que nous avons d'eux, que celle que
nous avons de nous-mêmes.*

What ordinarily prevents us from revealing the bottom of our
heart to our friends is not the diffidence we have for them, but
the diffidence we have for ourselves.

316 *Les personnes faibles ne peuvent être sincères.*

Weak people cannot be sincere.

317 *Ce n'est pas un grand malheur d'obliger des ingrats, mais c'en est un
insupportable d'être obligé à un malhonnête homme.*

It is not a great misfortune to oblige ingrates, but it is an insufferable one to be obliged to a dishonest man.

318 *On trouve des moyens pour guérir de la folie, mais on n'en trouve
point pour redresser un esprit de travers.*

One finds some means to cure folly, but one does not find any
to straighten a crooked mind.

319 On ne saurait conserver longtemps les sentiments qu'on doit avoir pour
ses amis et pour ses bienfaiteurs, si on se laisse la liberté de parler sou-
vent de leurs défauts.

One cannot preserve for long the sentiments one should have
for one's friends and for one's benefactors if one takes the liberty of speaking often of their shortcomings.

320 Louer les princes des vertus qu'ils n'ont pas, c'est leur dire impuné-
ment des injures.

To praise princes for virtues they do not have is to insult them
with impunity.

321 Nous sommes plus près d'aimer ceux qui nous haïssent que ceux qui
nous aiment plus que nous ne voulons.

We are closer to loving those who hate us than those who love
us more than we want.

322 Il n'y a que ceux qui sont méprisables qui craignent d'être méprisés.

Only those who are despicable fear being despised.

323 Notre sagesse n'est pas moins à la merci de la fortune que nos biens.

Our wisdom is no less at the mercy of fortune than our posses-
sions.

324 Il y a dans la jalousie plus d'amour-propre que d'amour.

There is in jealousy more self-love than love.

325 Nous nous consolons souvent par faiblesse des maux dont la raison n'a
pas la force de nous consoler.

We often console ourselves out of weakness for ills when reason
does not have the strength to console ourselves.

326 Le ridicule déshonore plus que le déshonneur.
Ridicule dishonors more than dishonor.

327 Nous n'avouons de petits défauts que pour persuader que nous n'en avons pas de grands.
We confess small shortcomings only in order to persuade others that we do not have any great ones.

328 L'envie est plus irréconciliable que la haine.
Envy is more irreconcilable than hatred.

329 On croit quelquefois haïr la flatterie, mais on ne hait que la manière de flatter.
One sometimes believes one hates flattery, but one only hates the manner of flattering.

330 On pardonne tant que l'on aime.
One forgives as long as one loves.

331 Il est plus difficile d'être fidèle à sa maîtresse quand on est heureux que quand on en est maltraité.
It is more difficult to be faithful to one's mistress when one is happy than when one is ill-treated by her.

332 Les femmes ne connaissent pas toute leur coquetterie.
Women do not know all of their coquetry.

333 Les femmes n'ont point de sévérité complète sans aversion.
Women do not have a complete severity without aversion.

334 Les femmes peuvent moins surmonter leur coquetterie que leur passion.
Women can less overcome their coquetry than their passion.

*335 Dans l'amour la tromperie va presque toujours plus loin que la mé-
fiance.*
In love, deception almost always goes further than mistrust.

336 Il y a une certaine sorte d'amour dont l'excès empêche la jalousie.
There is a certain sort of love the excess of which prevents jealousy.

*337 Il est de certaines bonnes qualités comme des sens ceux qui en sont
entièrement privés ne les peuvent apercevoir ni les comprendre.*
Certain good qualities share the same fate as the senses – those
who are entirely deprived of them can neither perceive them nor
understand them.

*338 Lorsque notre haine est trop vive, elle nous met au-dessous de ceux que
nous haïssons.*
When our hatred is too vivid, it places us below those we hate.

*339 Nous ne ressentons nos biens et nos maux qu'à proportion de notre
amour-propre.*
We feel our goods and ills only in proportion to our self-love.

*340 L'esprit de la plupart des femmes sert plus à fortifier leur folie que leur
raison.*
The minds of most women help strengthen their folly more
than their reason.

*341 Les passions de la jeunesse ne sont guère plus opposées au salut que la
tiédeur des vieilles gens.*
The passions of youth are hardly more opposed to salvation
than the lukewarmness of old people.

*342 L'accent du pays où l'on est né demeure dans l'esprit et dans le cœur,
comme dans le langage.*

342 The accent of the country where one was born remains in one's mind and heart, as in one's language.

343 *Pour être un grand homme, il faut savoir profiter de toute sa fortune.*
In order to be a great man, one needs to know how to profit from all of one's fortune.

344 *La plupart des hommes ont comme les plantes des propriétés cachées, que le hasard fait découvrir.*
Most men have, like plants, hidden properties, that chance discloses.

345 *Les occasions nous font connaître aux autres, et encore plus à nous-mêmes.*
Occasions make us known to others, and even more to ourselves.

346 *Il ne peut y avoir de règle dans l'esprit ni dans le cœur des femmes, si le tempérament n'en est d'accord.*
There cannot be any rule in the minds nor in the hearts of women if temperament is not in accord with it.

347 *Nous ne trouvons guère de gens de bon sens, que ceux qui sont de notre avis.*
We hardly find people of good sense, other than those who are of our opinion.

348 *Quand on aime, on doute souvent de ce qu'on croit le plus.*
When one loves, one often doubts what one believes the most.

349 *Le plus grand miracle de l'amour, c'est de guérir de la coquetterie.*
The greatest miracle of love is to cure coquetry.

350 Ce qui nous donne tant d'aigreur contre ceux qui nous font des finesses, c'est qu'ils croient être plus habiles que nous.

What makes us so bitter against those who attempt to outwit us is that they believe they are more clever than we are.

351 On a bien de la peine à rompre, quand on ne s'aime plus.

We have quite a hard time breaking up when we do not love each other anymore.

352 On s'ennuie presque toujours avec les gens avec qui il n'est pas permis de s'ennuyer.

One is almost always bored with the people with whom it is not permitted to be bored.

353 Un honnête homme peut être amoureux comme un fou, mais non pas comme un sot.

An honorable man may love like a madman, but not like a fool.

354 Il y a de certains défauts qui, bien mis en œuvre, brillent plus que la vertu même.

There are certain shortcomings which, when well brought into play, shine more than virtue itself.

355 On perd quelquefois des personnes qu'on regrette plus qu'on n'en est affligé; et d'autres dont on est affligé, et qu'on ne regrette guère.

One sometimes loses people whom one regrets more than grieves, and others whom one grieves, and hardly regrets.

356 Nous ne louons d'ordinaire de bon cœur que ceux qui nous admirent.

We ordinarily praise wholeheartedly only those who admire us.

357 Les petits esprits sont trop blessés des petites choses; les grands esprits les voient toutes, et n'en sont point blessés.

357 Small minds are hurt too much by small things; great minds see them all, and are not hurt by them.

358 *L'humilité est la véritable preuve des vertus chrétiennes: sans elle nous conservons tous nos défauts, et ils sont seulement couverts par l'orgueil qui les cache aux autres, et souvent à nous-mêmes.*
Humility is the true proof of Christian virtues: without it we preserve all our shortcomings, and they are only covered with pride which hides them from others, and often from ourselves.

359 *Les infidélités devraient éteindre l'amour, et il ne faudrait point être jaloux quand on a sujet de l'être. Il n'y a que les personnes qui évitent de donner de la jalousie qui soient dignes qu'on en ait pour elles.*
Infidelities should extinguish love, and one should not be jealous when one has reasons to be so. Only the people who avoid giving grounds for jealousy deserve it.

360 *On se décrie beaucoup plus auprès de nous par les moindres infidélités qu'on nous fait, que par les plus grandes qu'on fait aux autres.*
People fall in our esteem much more through the smallest infidelities they do to us than through the greater ones they do to others.

361 *La jalousie naît toujours avec l'amour, mais elle ne meurt pas toujours avec lui.*
Jealousy is always born with love, but it does not always die with it.

362 *La plupart des femmes ne pleurent pas tant la mort de leurs amants pour les avoir aimés, que pour paraître plus dignes d'être aimées.*
Most women bewail the death of their lovers less because they loved them, than to appear more worthy of being loved.

363 *Les violences qu'on nous fait nous font souvent moins de peine que celles que nous nous faisons à nous-mêmes.*

The violence done to us often gives us less pain than that which we do to ourselves.

364 *On sait assez qu'il ne faut guère parler de sa femme; mais on ne sait pas assez qu'on devrait encore moins parler de soi.*

It is known well enough that one should hardly talk about one's wife; but it is not known well enough that one should talk about oneself even less.

365 *Il y a de bonnes qualités qui dégénèrent en défauts quand elles sont naturelles, et d'autres qui ne sont jamais parfaites quand elles sont acquises. Il faut, par exemple, que la raison nous fasse ménagers de notre bien et de notre confiance; et il faut, au contraire, que la nature nous donne la bonté et la valeur.*

There are some good qualities which degenerate into shortcomings when they are natural, and others which are never perfect when they are acquired. It is necessary, for example, that reason make us manage our goods and our confidence; and it is necessary, on the contrary, that nature give us goodness and valor.

366 *Quelque défiance que nous ayons de la sincérité de ceux qui nous parlent, nous croyons toujours qu'ils nous disent plus vrai qu'aux autres.*

Whatever diffidence we have for the sincerity of those who speak to us, we always believe that they talk to us more truly than to others.

367 *Il y a peu d'honnêtes femmes qui ne soient lasses de leur métier.*

There are few honest women who are not weary of their trade.

368 *La plupart des honnêtes femmes sont des trésors cachés, qui ne sont en sûreté que parce qu'on ne les cherche pas.*

368 Most honest women are hidden treasures that are safe only because they are not sought.

369 *Les violences qu'on se fait pour s'empêcher d'aimer sont souvent plus cruelles que les rigueurs de ce qu'on aime.*
The violence one does to oneself to prevent oneself from loving is often more cruel than the harshness of those we love.

370 *Il n'y a guère de poltrons qui connaissent toujours toute leur peur.*
Hardly any cowards always know all their fears.

371 *C'est presque toujours la faute de celui qui aime de ne pas connaître quand on cesse de l'aimer.*
It is almost always the shortcoming of him who loves not to know when he is not loved anymore.

372 *La plupart des jeunes gens croient être naturels, lorsqu'ils ne sont que mal polis et grossiers.*
Most young people believe they are natural when they are only impolite and rude.

373 *Il y a de certaines larmes qui nous trompent souvent nous-mêmes après avoir trompé les autres.*
There are certain tears which often deceive us after having deceived others.

374 *Si on croit aimer sa maîtresse pour l'amour d'elle, on est bien trompé.*
If one believes one loves one's mistress for the sake of loving her, one is quite deceived.

375 *Les esprits médiocres condamnent d'ordinaire tout ce qui passe leur portée.*
Mediocre minds ordinarily condemn everything beyond their reach.

376 L'envie est détruite par la véritable amitié, et la coquetterie par le véritable amour.
Envy is destroyed by true friendship, and coquetry by true love.

377 Le plus grand défaut de la pénétration n'est pas de n'aller point jusqu'au but, c'est de le passer.
The greatest shortcoming of insight is not failing to reach the goal, but going past it.

378 On donne des conseils mais on n'inspire point de conduite.
One gives advice but one does not inspire conduct.

379 Quand notre mérite baisse, notre goût baisse aussi.
When our merit fails, our taste fails as well.

380 La fortune fait paraître nos vertus et nos vices, comme la lumière fait paraître les objets.
Fortune reveals our virtues and vices, as light reveals objects.

381 La violence qu'on se fait pour demeurer fidèle à ce qu'on aime ne vaut guère mieux qu'une infidélité.
The violence one does to oneself in order to remain faithful to what one loves is hardly worth more than infidelity.

382 Nos actions sont comme les bouts-rimés, que chacun fait rapporter à ce qu'il lui plaît.
Our actions are like set-rhymes which everyone relates to what he likes.

383 L'envie de parler de nous, et de faire voir nos défauts du côté que nous voulons bien les montrer, fait une grande partie de notre sincérité.
The desire to talk about ourselves, and to show our shortcomings in the light in which we agree to show them, is a great part of our sincerity.

384 On ne devrait s'étonner que de pouvoir encore s'étonner.
One should only be surprised at still being able to be surprised.

385 On est presque également difficile à contenter quand on a beaucoup d'amour et quand on n'en a plus guère.
We are almost equally difficult to satisfy when we have a lot of love and when we hardly have any more.

386 Il n'y a point de gens qui aient plus souvent tort que ceux qui ne peuvent souffrir d'en avoir.
No people are more often wrong than those who cannot stand to be so.

387 Un sot n'a pas assez d'étoffe pour être bon.
A fool is not cut out to be good.

388 Si la vanité ne renverse pas entièrement les vertus, du moins elle les ébranle toutes.
If vanity does not entirely overthrow the virtues, at least it unsettles them all.

389 Ce qui nous rend la vanité des autres insupportable, c'est qu'elle blesse la nôtre.
What makes the vanity of others insufferable is that it hurts our own.

390 On renonce plus aisément à son intérêt qu'à son goût.
One more easily renounces one's self-interest than one's taste.

391 La fortune ne paraît jamais si aveugle qu'à ceux à qui elle ne fait pas de bien.
Fortune never appears so blind as to those to whom she does not do any good.

392 *Il faut gouverner la fortune comme la santé: en jouir quand elle est bonne, prendre patience quand elle est mauvaise, et ne faire jamais de grands remèdes sans un extrême besoin.*

It is necessary to govern fortune like health: to enjoy her when she is good, to be patient when she is bad, and never to provide great remedies without an extreme need.

393 *L'air bourgeois se perd quelquefois à l'armée; mais il ne se perd jamais à la cour.*

The look of the bourgeois is sometimes lost in the army, but it is never lost at court.

394 *On peut être plus fin qu'un autre, mais non pas plus fin que tous les autres.*

One can be smarter than someone else, but one cannot be smarter than everyone else.

395 *On est quelquefois moins malheureux d'être trompé de ce qu'on aime, que d'en être détrompé.*

One is sometimes less unhappy to be deceived about what one loves, than to be undeceived about it.

396 *On garde longtemps son premier amant, quand on n'en prend point de second.*

One keeps one's first lover for a long time, when one does not take a second one.

397 *Nous n'avons pas le courage de dire en général que nous n'avons point de défauts, et que nos ennemis n'ont point de bonnes qualités; mais en détail nous ne sommes pas trop éloignés de le croire.*

We do not have the courage to say in general that we do not have any shortcomings, and that our enemies do not have any good qualities; but we are not too far from believing it as to the details.

98 De tous nos défauts, celui dont nous demeurons le plus aisément d'accord, c'est de la paresse; nous nous persuadons qu'elle tient à toutes les vertus paisibles et que, sans détruire entièrement les autres, elle en suspend seulement les fonctions.

Of all our shortcomings, the one with which we most easily live in agreement is laziness; we persuade ourselves that it pertains to all of the peaceful virtues, and that, without entirely destroying the others, it only suspends their functions.

399 Il y a une élévation qui ne dépend point de la fortune: c'est un certain air qui nous distingue et qui semble nous destiner aux grandes choses; c'est un prix que nous nous donnons imperceptiblement à nous-mêmes; c'est par cette qualité que nous usurpons les déférences des autres hommes, et c'est elle d'ordinaire qui nous met plus au-dessus d'eux que la naissance, les dignités, et le mérite même.

There is an eminence which does not depend upon fortune: it is a certain bearing which distinguishes us and which seems to destine us to great things; it is a price that we imperceptibly set upon ourselves; it is by this quality that we usurp the deference of other men, and it is that, ordinarily, which places us above them more than birth, high rank, and merit itself.

400 Il y a du mérite sans élévation, mais il n'y a point d'élévation sans quelque mérite.

There is merit without eminence, but there is no eminence without some merit.

401 L'élévation est au mérite ce que la parure est aux belles personnes.

Eminence is to merit what adornments are to beautiful people.

402 Ce qui se trouve le moins dans la galanterie, c'est de l'amour.

What one finds least in love affairs is love.

403 *La fortune se sert quelquefois de nos défauts pour nous élever, et il y a des gens incommodes dont le mérite serait mal récompensé si on ne voulait acheter leur absence.*

Fortune sometimes uses our shortcomings to elevate us, and there are troublesome people whose merit would be badly rewarded if one did not want to buy their absence.

404 *Il semble que la nature ait caché dans le fond de notre esprit des talents et une habileté que nous ne connaissons pas; les passions seules ont le droit de les mettre au jour, et de nous donner quelquefois des vues plus certaines et plus achevées que l'art ne saurait faire.*

It seems that nature has hidden in the bottom of our mind some talents and a cleverness that we do not know; the passions alone have the right to bring them to light, and sometimes to give us views that are more certain and more accomplished than art could do.

405 *Nous arrivons tout nouveaux aux divers âges de la vie, et nous y manquons souvent d'expérience malgré le nombre des années.*

We arrive totally new at the various stages of life, and there we often lack experience, despite the number of our years.

406 *Les coquettes se font honneur d'être jalouses de leurs amants, pour cacher qu'elles sont envieuses des autres femmes.*

Coquettish women pride themselves on being jealous of their lovers to hide that they are envious of other women.

407 *Il s'en faut bien que ceux qui s'attrapent à nos finesses ne nous paraissent aussi ridicules que nous nous le paraissons à nous-mêmes quand les finesses des autres nous ont attrapés.*

Those who are tricked by our shrewdness are very far from appearing to us as ridiculous as we appear to ourselves when the shrewdness of others has tricked us.

408 Le plus dangereux ridicule des vieilles personnes qui ont été aimables, c'est d'oublier qu'elles ne le sont plus.

The most dangerous ridicule of old people who have been amiable is to forget that they are no longer so.

409 Nous aurions souvent honte de nos plus belles actions si le monde voyait tous les motifs qui les produisent.

We would often be ashamed of our most beautiful actions if everyone saw the motives that produced them.

410 Le plus grand effort de l'amitié n'est pas de montrer nos défauts à un ami; c'est de lui faire voir les siens.

The greatest task of friendship is not to show our shortcomings to a friend; it is to show him his own.

411 On n'a guère de défauts qui ne soient plus pardonnables que les moyens dont on se sert pour les cacher.

One hardly has any shortcomings which are not more forgivable than the means one uses to hide them.

412 Quelque honte que nous ayons méritée, il est presque toujours en notre pouvoir de rétablir notre réputation.

Whatever shame we have deserved, it is almost always in our power to restore our reputation.

413 On ne plaît pas longtemps quand on n'a que d'une sorte d'esprit.

One does not please for long when one has only a certain turn of mind.

414 Les fous et les sottes gens ne voient que par leur humeur.

Mad and foolish people see only through their humors.

415 L'esprit nous sert quelquefois à faire hardiment des sottises.

The mind sometimes helps us boldly do foolish things.

416 La vivacité qui augmente en vieillissant ne va pas loin de la folie.
That vivacity which increases with age does not go far from folly.

417 En amour celui qui est guéri le premier est toujours le mieux guéri.
In love, the first cured is always the best cured.

418 Les jeunes femmes qui ne veulent point paraître coquettes, et les hommes d'un âge avancé qui ne veulent pas être ridicules, ne doivent jamais parler de l'amour comme d'une chose où ils puissent avoir part.
Young women who do not want to appear coquettish, and men of an advanced age who do not want to be ridiculous, must never speak of love as a thing in which they can have a share.

419 Nous pouvons paraître grands dans un emploi au-dessous de notre mérite, mais nous paraissons souvent petits dans un emploi plus grand que nous.
We can appear great in an occupation beneath our merit, but we often appear small in an occupation greater than us.

420 Nous croyons souvent avoir de la constance dans les malheurs, lorsque nous n'avons que de l'abattement, et nous les souffrons sans oser les regarder comme les poltrons se laissent tuer de peur de se défendre.
We often believe we have constancy in misfortunes, whereas we only have despondency; and we endure them without daring to look at them, like cowards who let themselves be killed for fear of defending themselves.

421 La confiance fournit plus à la conversation que l'esprit.
Trust contributes more to conversation than wit.

422 Toutes les passions nous font faire des fautes, mais l'amour nous en fait faire de plus ridicules.

422 All the passions make us make mistakes, but love makes us make the most ridiculous ones.

423 *Peu de gens savent être vieux.*
Few people know how to be old.

424 *Nous nous faisons honneur des défauts opposés à ceux que nous avons: quand nous sommes faibles, nous nous vantons d'être opiniâtres.*
We pride ourselves on the shortcomings opposite to those that we have: when we are weak, we boast of being obstinate.

425 *La pénétration a un air de deviner qui flatte plus notre vanité que toutes les autres qualités de l'esprit.*
Insight has a way to divine which flatters our vanity more than all of the other qualities of mind.

426 *La grâce de la nouveauté et la longue habitude, quelque opposées qu'elles soient, nous empêchent également de sentir les défauts de nos amis.*
Long habit and the grace of novelty, however opposed they may be, equally prevent us from feeling the shortcomings of our friends.

427 *La plupart des amis dégoûtent de l'amitié, et la plupart des dévots dégoûtent de la dévotion.*
Most friends leave one disgusted with friendship, and most devout people leave one disgusted with devotion.

428 *Nous pardonnons aisément à nos amis les défauts qui ne nous regardent pas.*
We easily forgive our friends for shortcomings which are of no concern to us.

429 *Les femmes qui aiment pardonnent plus aisément les grandes indiscrétions que les petites infidélités.*

Women who love forgive more easily great indiscretions than small infidelities.

430 *Dans la vieillesse de l'amour comme dans celle de l'âge on vit encore pour les maux, mais on ne vit plus pour les plaisirs.*

In the old age of love as in that of life, one still lives for the ills, but one no longer lives for the pleasures.

431 *Rien n'empêche tant d'être naturel que l'envie de le paraître.*

Nothing prevents one from being natural as much as the desire to appear to be so.

432 *C'est en quelque sorte se donner part aux belles actions, que de les louer de bon cœur.*

Praising beautiful actions wholeheartedly is in some way giving oneself a share in them.

433 *La plus véritable marque d'être né avec de grandes qualités, c'est d'être né sans envie.*

The truest mark of being born with great qualities is to be born without envy.

434 *Quand nos amis nous ont trompés, on ne doit que de l'indifférence aux marques de leur amitié, mais on doit toujours de la sensibilité à leurs malheurs.*

When our friends have deceived us, we only owe indifference to the tokens of their friendship, but we always owe some sensibility to their misfortunes.

435 *La fortune et l'humeur gouvernent le monde.*
Fortune and humors govern the world.

436 *Il est plus aisé de connaître l'homme en général que de connaître un homme en particulier.*
It is easier to know man in general than to know a man in particular.

437 *On ne doit pas juger du mérite d'un homme par ses grandes qualités, mais par l'usage qu'il en sait faire.*
One should not judge of a man's merit by his great qualities, but by the use to which he knows how to put them.

438 *Il y a une certaine reconnaissance vive qui ne nous acquitte pas seulement des bienfaits que nous avons reçus, mais qui fait même que nos amis nous doivent en leur payant ce que nous leur devons.*
There is a certain vivid gratitude which not only repays another for the benefits we have received, but which even makes our friends owe us what we owe them when we pay them.

439 *Nous ne désirerions guère de choses avec ardeur, si nous connaissions parfaitement ce que nous désirons.*
We would hardly desire anything with ardor if we knew perfectly what we desire.

440 *Ce qui fait que la plupart des femmes sont peu touchées de l'amitié, c'est qu'elle est fade quand on a senti de l'amour.*
The reason most women are little touched by friendship is that it is dull after one has felt love.

441 *Dans l'amitié comme dans l'amour on est souvent plus heureux par les choses qu'on ignore que par celles que l'on sait.*

441 In friendship as in love, one is often happier from the things one does not know than from those one does.

442 *Nous essayons de nous faire honneur des défauts que nous ne voulons pas corriger.*
We try to pride ourselves on the shortcomings we do not want to correct.

443 *Les passions les plus violentes nous laissent quelquefois du relâche, mais la vanité nous agite toujours.*
The most violent passions sometimes give us some respite, but vanity always agitates us.

444 *Les vieux fous sont plus fous que les jeunes.*
Old fools are more foolish than young ones.

445 *La faiblesse est plus opposée à la vertu que le vice.*
Weakness is more opposed to virtue than vice.

446 *Ce qui rend les douleurs de la honte et de la jalousie si aiguës, c'est que la vanité ne peut servir à les supporter.*
What makes the pains of shame and of jealousy so sharp, is that vanity cannot help one to bear them.

447 *La bienséance est la moindre de toutes les lois, et la plus suivie.*
Decency is the least of all laws, and the most followed.

448 *Un esprit droit a moins de peine de se soumettre aux esprits de travers que de les conduire.*
An upright mind has less difficulty submitting itself to crooked minds than guiding them.

449 *Lorsque la fortune nous surprend en nous donnant une grande place sans nous y avoir conduits par degrés, ou sans que nous nous y soyons élevés par nos espérances, il est presque impossible de s'y bien soutenir, et de paraître digne de l'occuper.*

When fortune surprises us by giving us a great position without having guided us to it by degrees, or without our having raised ourselves to it through our hopes, it is almost impossible for us to fill this position well, and to appear worthy of occupying it.

450 *Notre orgueil s'augmente souvent de ce que nous retranchons de nos autres défauts.*

Our pride is often increased by what we withdraw from our other shortcomings.

451 *Il n'y a point de sots si incommodes que ceux qui ont de l'esprit.*

There are no fools as inconvenient as those who have wit.

452 *Il n'y a point d'homme qui se croie en chacune de ses qualités au-dessous de l'homme du monde qu'il estime le plus.*

There is no man who believes that each of his qualities is beneath the man he esteems most in the world.[5]

453 *Dans les grandes affaires on doit moins s'appliquer à faire naître des occasions qu'à profiter de celles qui se présentent.*

In great affairs one should apply oneself less to giving birth to occasions than to profiting from those that present themselves.

454 *Il n'y a guère d'occasion où l'on fit un méchant marché de renoncer au bien qu'on dit de nous, à condition de n'en dire point de mal.*

There are hardly any occasions in which we make a bad bargain

5   This maxim admits of another translation: "There is no man who believes that each of his qualities is beneath the man of the world he esteems most."

by renouncing the good being told about us, provided that no ill is said either.

455 *Quelque disposition qu'ait le monde à mal juger, il fait encore plus souvent grâce au faux mérite qu'il ne fait injustice au véritable.*
Whatever disposition the world has to judge badly, it still pardons false merit more often than it does injustice to true merit.

456 *On est quelquefois un sot avec de l'esprit, mais on ne l'est jamais avec du jugement.*
One is sometimes a fool with some wit, but one is never so with judgment.

457 *Nous gagnerions plus de nous laisser voir tels que nous sommes, que d'essayer de paraître ce que nous ne sommes pas.*
We would gain more by letting ourselves be seen as we are, than by trying to appear as what we are not.

458 *Nos ennemis approchent plus de la vérité dans les jugements qu'ils font de nous que nous n'en approchons nous-mêmes.*
Our enemies come closer to the truth in the judgments they pass on us than we do ourselves.

459 *Il y a plusieurs remèdes qui guérissent de l'amour, mais il n'y en a point d'infaillibles.*
There are several remedies which cure love, but none is infallible.

460 *Il s'en faut bien que nous connaissions tout ce que nos passions nous font faire.*
We are very far from knowing all that our passions make us do.

461 *La vieillesse est un tyran qui défend sur peine de la vie tous les plaisirs de la jeunesse.*

461 Old age is a tyrant who forbids under pain of death all the pleasures of youth.

462 *Le même orgueil qui nous fait blâmer les défauts dont nous nous croyons exempts, nous porte à mépriser les bonnes qualités que nous n'avons pas.*
The very pride which makes us blame the shortcomings from which we believe we are exempt, induces us to despise the good qualities we do not have.

463 *Il y a souvent plus d'orgueil que de bonté à plaindre les malheurs de nos ennemis; c'est pour leur faire sentir que nous sommes au-dessus d'eux que nous leur donnons des marques de compassion.*
There is often more pride than goodness in pitying the misfortunes of our enemies; it is in order to make them feel that we are above them that we give them tokens of compassion.

464 *Il y a un excès de biens et de maux qui passe notre sensibilité.*
There is an excess of goods and ills that goes past our sensibility.

465 *Il s'en faut bien que l'innocence ne trouve autant de protection que le crime.*
Innocence is very far from finding as much protection as crime does.

466 *De toutes les passions violentes, celle qui sied le moins mal aux femmes, c'est l'amour.*
Of all violent passions, the one which is ill-becoming to women is love.

467 *La vanité nous fait faire plus de choses contre notre goût que la raison.*
Vanity makes us do more things against our taste than reason does.

468 *Il y a de méchantes qualités qui font de grands talents.*
There are some bad qualities which make great talents.

469 *On ne souhaite jamais ardemment ce qu'on ne souhaite que par rai-son.*
One never ardently wishes what one only wishes from reason.

470 *Toutes nos qualités sont incertaines et douteuses en bien comme en mal, et elles sont presque toutes à la merci des occasions.*
All our qualities, both good and bad, are uncertain and doubt-ful, and almost all of them are at the mercy of the occasion.

471 *Dans les premières passions les femmes aiment l'amant, et dans les autres elles aiment l'amour.*
In the first passions, women love the lover, and in the others they love love.

472 *L'orgueil a ses bizarreries, comme les autres passions; on a honte d'avouer que l'on ait de la jalousie, et on se fait honneur d'en avoir eu, et d'être capable d'en avoir.*
Pride has its oddities, like the other passions; we are ashamed to confess that we are jealous, and we pride ourselves on having been so, and on being capable of being so.

473 *Quelque rare que soit le véritable amour, il l'est encore moins que la véritable amitié.*
However rare true love may be, it is still less rare than true friendship.

474 *Il y a peu de femmes dont le mérite dure plus que la beauté.*
There are few women whose merit outlasts their beauty.

475 *L'envie d'être plaint, ou d'être admiré, fait souvent la plus grande partie de notre confiance.*

475 The desire to be pitied, or to be admired, often constitutes the greatest part of our trust.

476 *Notre envie dure toujours plus longtemps que le bonheur de ceux que nous envions.*
Our envy always lasts longer than the happiness of those we envy.

477 *La même fermeté qui sert à résister à l'amour sert aussi à le rendre violent et durable, et les personnes faibles qui sont toujours agitées des passions n'en sont presque jamais véritablement remplies.*
The same strength which helps to resist love also helps to render it violent and lasting; and the weak people who are always agitated by the passions are almost never truly filled by them.

478 *L'imagination ne saurait inventer tant de diverses contrariétés qu'il y en a naturellement dans le cœur de chaque personne.*
The imagination cannot invent as many various contrarieties as there are naturally in the heart of each person.

479 *Il n'y a que les personnes qui ont de la fermeté qui puissent avoir une véritable douceur; celles qui paraissent douces n'ont d'ordinaire que de la faiblesse, qui se convertit aisément en aigreur.*
Only the people with strength can have true kindness; those who appear kind ordinarily only have weakness, which easily turns into bitterness.

480 *La timidité est un défaut dont il est dangereux de reprendre les personnes qu'on en veut corriger.*
Timidity is a shortcoming which it is dangerous to reprimand in those whom one wants to correct it.

481 *Rien n'est plus rare que la véritable bonté; ceux mêmes qui croient en avoir n'ont d'ordinaire que de la complaisance ou de la faiblesse.*

481 Nothing is rarer than true goodness; the very people who believe they are good are ordinarily only accommodating or weak.

482 *L'esprit s'attache par paresse et par constance à ce qui lui est facile ou agréable; cette habitude met toujours des bornes à nos connaissances, et jamais personne ne s'est donné la peine d'étendre et de conduire son esprit aussi loin qu'il pourrait aller.*
The mind binds itself through laziness and through constancy to that which is easy or agreeable; this habit always limits our knowledge, and no one ever took pains to stretch and guide one's mind as far as it could go.

483 *On est d'ordinaire plus médisant par vanité que par malice.*
One ordinarily slanders more out of vanity than out of malice.

484 *Quand on a le cœur encore agité par les restes d'une passion, on est plus près d'en prendre une nouvelle que quand on est entièrement guéri.*
When one's heart is still agitated by the remains of a passion, one is closer to taking up a new one than when one is entirely cured from it.

485 *Ceux qui ont eu de grandes passions se trouvent toute leur vie heureux, et malheureux, d'en être guéris.*
Those who have had great passions find themselves for the rest of their lives happy, and unhappy to have been cured of them.

486 *Il y a encore plus de gens sans intérêt que sans envie.*
There are even more people without self-interest than without envy.

487 *Nous avons plus de paresse dans l'esprit que dans le corps.*
We have more laziness in the mind than in the body.

488 Le calme ou l'agitation de notre humeur ne dépend pas tant de ce qui nous arrive de plus considérable dans la vie, que d'un arrangement commode ou désagréable de petites choses qui arrivent tous les jours.

The calm or the agitation of our humors does not depend so much on the most considerable events in life, as on a convenient or disagreeable arrangement of small things that happen every day.

489 Quelque méchants que soient les hommes, ils n'oseraient paraître enne- mis de la vertu, et lorsqu'ils la veulent persécuter, ils feignent de croire qu'elle est fausse ou ils lui supposent des crimes.

However mean men may be, they dare not appear as enemies of virtue; and when they want to persecute it, they feign to believe that it is false or that they credit it with crimes.

490 On passe souvent de l'amour à l'ambition, mais on ne revient guère de l'ambition à l'amour.

One often passes from love to ambition, but one hardly comes back from ambition to love.

491 L'extrême avarice se méprend presque toujours; il n'y a point de pas- sion qui s'éloigne plus souvent de son but, ni sur qui le présent ait tant de pouvoir au préjudice de l'avenir.

Extreme avarice is almost always mistaken; there is no passion which wanders more often from its goal, nor any over which the present has so much power to the detriment of the future.

492 L'avarice produit souvent des effets contraires; il y a un nombre infi- ni de gens qui sacrifient tout leur bien à des espérances douteuses et éloignées, d'autres méprisent de grands avantages à venir pour de petits intérêts présents.

Avarice often produces contrary effects; there is an infinite number of people who sacrifice all their goods to dubious and far away hopes; others despise great future advantages for petty present interests.

493 *Il semble que les hommes ne se trouvent pas assez de défauts; ils en augmentent encore le nombre par de certaines qualités singulières dont ils affectent de se parer, et ils les cultivent avec tant de soin qu'elles deviennent à la fin des défauts naturels, qu'il ne dépend plus d'eux de corriger.*

It seems that men do not find themselves having enough shortcomings; they still increase their number with certain peculiar qualities with which they affect to adorn themselves, and they cultivate them with so much care that they finally become natural shortcomings, which they can no longer correct.

494 *Ce qui fait voir que les hommes connaissent mieux leurs fautes qu'on ne pense, c'est qu'ils n'ont jamais tort quand on les entend parler de leur conduite: le même amour-propre qui les aveugle d'ordinaire les éclaire alors, et leur donne des vues si justes qu'il leur fait supprimer ou déguiser les moindres choses qui peuvent être condamnées.*

A sign that men know their shortcomings better than one thinks is that they are never wrong when they talk about their conduct: the same self-love which ordinarily blinds them then enlightens them, and gives them views that are so just that it makes them suppress or disguise the smallest things which can be condemned.

495 *Il faut que les jeunes gens qui entrent dans le monde soient honteux ou étourdis: un air capable et composé se tourne d'ordinaire en impertinence.*

It is necessary that the young people who enter into the world be shameful or scatterbrained; a capable and composed bearing ordinarily turns into impertinence.

496 Les querelles ne dureraient pas longtemps, si le tort n'était que d'un côté.

Quarrels would not last long if the blame were only on one side.

497 Il ne sert de rien d'être jeune sans être belle, ni d'être belle sans être jeune.

It is of no use for a woman to be young without being beautiful, or to be beautiful without being young.

498 Il y a des personnes si légères et si frivoles qu'elles sont aussi éloignées d'avoir de véritables défauts que des qualités solides.

There are some people who are so lighthearted and so frivolous, that they are as remote from having true shortcomings as from having sound qualities.

499 On ne compte d'ordinaire la première galanterie des femmes que lorsqu'elles en ont une seconde.

We ordinarily reckon the first love affair of women only when they have a second one.

500 Il y a des gens si remplis d'eux-mêmes que, lorsqu'ils sont amoureux, ils trouvent moyen d'être occupés de leur passion sans l'être de la personne qu'ils aiment.

There are people so full of themselves that, when they are in love, they manage to be taken by their passion and not by the person they love.

501 L'amour, tout agréable qu'il est, plaît encore plus par les manières dont il se montre que par lui-même.

Love, agreeable as it is, pleases even more by the ways in which it appears than by itself.

502 Peu d'esprit avec de la droiture ennuie moins, à la longue, que beaucoup d'esprit avec du travers.

502 Little wit with rectitude bores less, in the long run, than much wit with crookedness.

503 *La jalousie est le plus grand de tous les maux, et celui qui fait le moins de pitié aux personnes qui le causent.*
Jealousy is the greatest of all evils, and the one which least arouses pity in the people who cause it.

504 *Après avoir parlé de la fausseté de tant de vertus apparentes, il est raisonnable de dire quelque chose de la fausseté du mépris de la mort. J'entends parler de ce mépris de la mort que les païens se vantent de tirer de leurs propres forces, sans l'espérance d'une meilleure vie. Il y a différence entre souffrir la mort constamment, et la mépriser. Le premier est assez ordinaire; mais je crois que l'autre n'est jamais sincère. On a écrit néanmoins tout ce qui peut le plus persuader que la mort n'est point un mal; et les hommes les plus faibles aussi bien que les héros ont donné mille exemples célèbres pour établir cette opinion. Cependant je doute que personne de bon sens l'ait jamais cru; et la peine que l'on prend pour le persuader aux autres et à soi-même fait assez voir que cette entreprise n'est pas aisée. On peut avoir divers sujets de dégoût dans la vie, mais on n'a jamais raison de mépriser la mort; ceux mêmes qui se la donnent volontairement ne la comptent pas pour si peu de chose, et ils s'en étonnent et la rejettent comme les autres, lorsqu'elle vient à eux par une autre voie que celle qu'ils ont choisie. L'inégalité que l'on remarque dans le courage d'un nombre infini de vaillants hommes vient de ce que la mort se découvre différemment à leur imagination, et y paraît plus présente en un temps qu'en un autre. Ainsi il arrive qu'après avoir méprisé ce qu'ils ne connaissent pas, ils craignent enfin ce qu'ils connaissent. Il faut éviter de l'envisager avec toutes ses circonstances, si on ne veut pas croire qu'elle soit le plus grand de tous les maux. Les plus habiles et les plus braves sont ceux qui prennent de plus honnêtes prétextes pour s'empêcher de la considérer. Mais tout homme qui la sait voir telle qu'elle est, trouve que c'est*

une chose épouvantable. La nécessité de mourir faisait toute la constance des philosophes. Ils croyaient qu'il fallait aller de bonne grâce où l'on ne saurait s'empêcher d'aller; et, ne pouvant éterniser leur vie, il n'y avait rien qu'ils ne fissent pour éterniser leur réputation, et sauver du naufrage ce qui n'en peut être garanti. Contentons-nous pour faire bonne mine de ne nous pas dire à nous-mêmes tout ce que nous en pensons, et espérons plus de notre tempérament que de ces faibles raisonnements qui nous font croire que nous pouvons approcher de la mort avec indifférence. La gloire de mourir avec fermeté, l'es-pérance d'être regretté, le désir de laisser une belle réputation, l'assurance d'être affranchi des misères de la vie, et de ne dépendre plus des caprices de la fortune, sont des remèdes qu'on ne doit pas rejeter. Mais on ne doit pas croire aussi qu'ils soient infaillibles. Ils font pour nous assurer ce qu'une simple haie fait souvent à la guerre pour assurer ceux qui doivent approcher d'un lieu d'où l'on tire. Quand on en est éloigné, on s'imagine qu'elle peut mettre à couvert; mais quand on en est proche, on trouve que c'est un faible secours. C'est nous flatter, de croire que la mort nous paraisse de près ce que nous en avons jugé de loin, et que nos sentiments, qui ne sont que faiblesse, soient d'une trempe assez forte pour ne point souffrir d'atteinte par la plus rude de toutes les épreuves. C'est aussi mal connaître les effets de l'amour-propre, que de penser qu'il puisse nous aider à compter pour rien ce qui le doit nécessairement détruire, et la raison, dans laquelle on croit trouver tant de ressources, est trop faible en cette rencontre pour nous persuader ce que nous voulons. C'est elle au contraire qui nous trahit le plus souvent, et qui, au lieu de nous inspirer le mépris de la mort, sert à nous découvrir ce qu'elle a d'affreux et de terrible. Tout ce qu'elle peut faire pour nous est de nous conseiller d'en détourner les yeux pour les arrêter sur d'autres objets. Caton et Brutus en choisirent d'illustres. Un laquais se contenta il y a quelque temps de danser sur l'échafaud où il allait être roué. Ainsi, bien que les motifs soient différents, ils produisent les mêmes effets. De sorte qu'il est vrai que, quelque disproportion qu'il y ait entre les grands hommes et les gens du commun, on a vu mille fois les uns et les autres recevoir la mort d'un même visage; mais ç'a tou-jours été avec cette différence que, dans le mépris que les grands hommes font paraître pour la mort, c'est l'amour de la gloire qui leur en ôte la vue, et dans les gens du commun ce n'est qu'un effet de leur peu de lumière qui les empêche de connaître la grandeur de leur mal et leur laisse la liberté de penser à autre chose.

504 After having spoken about the falseness of so many apparent virtues, it is reasonable to say something about the falseness of the contempt for death. I want to speak about this contempt for death which the pagans boast of deriving from their own strength, without the hope of a better life. There is a difference between steadfastly enduring death and having contempt for it. The first is quite ordinary, but I believe that the other is never sincere. Yet, everything has been written which can best per-suade us that death is not an evil; and the weakest men, as well as heroes, have provided a thousand famous examples to estab-lish this opinion. However, I doubt that anybody with good sense ever believed it; and the difficulty in persuading others and oneself of it shows well-enough that this undertaking is not easy. One can have various objects of disgust in life, but one is never right to have contempt for death. Those very ones who willingly give themselves to death do not count it as so little a thing, and, when it comes to them by a way other than the one they have chosen, they are frightened by it and reject it like the others do. The inequality that we notice in the courage of an infinite number of valiant men comes from death's revealing itself differently to their imaginations, and appears more vivid at one time than at another. Thus, it happens that after having had contempt for what they do not know, they finally fear what they do know. It is necessary to avoid imagining it in all of its particulars if one does not want to believe that it is the greatest of all evils. The most clever and the most brave are those who find more honest pretexts to prevent themselves from consider-

ing it. But any man who knows how to see it as it is finds that it is a dreadful thing. The necessity of dying caused all the constancy of philosophers. They believed that one had to go willingly where one could not prevent oneself from going; and, unable to make their lives eternal, there was nothing they did not do to make their reputations eternal, and to save from the shipwreck what there is no guarantee of saving. Let us content ourselves in order to bear it well, not to tell ourselves all we think about it; and let us hope for more from our temperament than from that weak reasoning which makes us believe that we can approach death with indifference. The glory of dying with resolve, the hope of being regretted, the desire to leave a fine reputation, the assurance of being freed from the miseries of life, and not having to depend anymore on the caprices of fortune, are remedies that one should not cast away. But one should also not believe that these remedies are infallible. They reassure us like a simple hedgerow often reassures those in war who must approach a place from which people are shooting. When one is far off, one imagines that it can protect one; but when one is close to it, one finds it of little help. We flatter ourselves when we believe that death appears to be from close-up what we judged it to be from afar, and that our sentiments, which are only weaknesses, are of a steely enough quality not to suffer a blow from the roughest of all trials. It is also to know badly the effects of self-love, to think that it can help us consider as nothing that which must necessarily destroy it; and reason, in which one believes one finds so many resources, is too weak in this encounter to persuade us of what we want. On the contrary, it is reason which betrays us most often, and, which, instead of inspiring us with the contempt for death, helps us discover what is frightful and terrible to it. All reason can do for us is to advise us to turn our eyes away from death in order to have them rest upon other objects. Cato and Brutus chose some illustrious ones. A lackey was satisfied some time ago with dancing on the scaffold upon which he was about to be broken on the wheel. Thus, even though the motives are different, they produce the same effects. So that it is true that, whatever disproportion there is between great men and common people, one has seen a thousand times the one and the other receive death with the same face. But there has always been this difference that, in the contempt that great men show for death, it is the love of glory which takes their view away from it, and in common people, it is only an effect of their meager enlightenment which prevents them from knowing the magnitude of their affliction and allows them the liberty to think about something else.

Avis au lecteur
(1665)

Voici un portrait du cœur de l'homme que je donne au public, sous le nom de *Réflexions ou Maximes morales*. Il court fortune de ne plaire pas à tout le monde, parce qu'on trouvera peut-être qu'il ressemble trop, et qu'il ne flatte pas assez. Il y a apparence que l'intention du peintre n'a jamais été de faire paraître cet ouvrage, et qu'il serait encore renfermé dans son cabinet si une méchante copie qui en a couru, et qui a passé même depuis quelque temps en Hollande, n'avait obligé un de ses amis de m'en donner une autre, qu'il dit être tout à fait conforme à l'original; mais toute correcte qu'elle est, possible n'évitera-t-elle pas la censure de certaines personnes qui ne peuvent souffrir que l'on se mêle de pénétrer dans le fond de leur cœur, et qui croient être en droit d'empêcher que les autres les connaissent, parce qu'elles ne veulent pas se connaître elles-mêmes. Il est vrai que, comme ces *Maximes* sont remplies de ces sortes de vérités dont l'orgueil humain ne se peut accommoder, il est presque impossible qu'il ne se soulève contre elles, et qu'elles ne s'attirent des censeurs. Aussi est-ce pour eux que je mets ici une *Lettre* que l'on m'a donnée, qui a été faite depuis que le manuscrit a paru, et dans le temps que chacun se mêlait d'en dire son avis. Elle m'a semblé assez propre pour répondre aux principales difficultés que l'on peut opposer aux *Réflexions*, et pour expliquer les sentiments de leur auteur. Elle suffit pour faire voir que ce qu'elles contiennent n'est autre chose que l'abrégé d'une morale conforme aux pensées de

96

plusieurs Pères de l'Église, et que celui qui les a écrites a eu beaucoup de raison de croire qu'il ne pouvait s'égarer en suivant de si bons guides, et qu'il lui était permis de parler de l'*homme* comme les Pères en ont parlé. Mais si le respect qui leur est dû n'est pas capable de retenir le chagrin des critiques, s'ils ne font point de scrupule de condamner l'opinion de ces grands hommes en condamnant ce livre, je prie le lecteur de ne les pas imiter, de ne laisser point entraîner son esprit au premier mouvement de son cœur, et de donner ordre, s'il est possible, que l'*amour-propre* ne se mêle point dans le jugement qu'il en fera; car s'il le consulte, il ne faut pas s'attendre qu'il puisse être favorable à ces *Maximes*: comme elles traitent l'*amour-propre* de corrupteur de la raison, il ne manquera pas de prévenir l'esprit contre elles. Il faut donc prendre garde que cette prévention ne les justifie, et se persuader qu'il n'y a rien de plus propre à établir la vérité de ces *Réflexions* que la chaleur et la subtilité que l'on témoignera pour les combattre. En effet il sera difficile de faire croire à tout homme de bon sens que l'on les condamne par d'autre motif que par celui de l'intérêt caché, de l'orgueil et de l'amour-propre. En un mot, le meilleur parti que le lecteur ait à prendre est de se mettre d'abord dans l'esprit qu'il n'y a aucune de ces maximes qui le regarde en particulier, et qu'il en est seul excepté, bien qu'elles paraissent générales; après cela, je lui réponds qu'il sera le premier à y souscrire, et qu'il croira qu'elles font encore grâce au cœur humain. Voilà ce que j'avais à dire sur cet écrit en général. Pour ce qui est de la méthode que l'on y eût pu observer, je crois qu'il eût été à désirer que chaque *maxime* eût eu un titre du sujet qu'elle traite, et qu'elles eussent été mises dans un plus grand ordre; mais je ne l'ai pu faire sans renverser entièrement celui de la copie qu'on m'a donnée; et comme il y a plusieurs *maximes* sur une même matière, ceux à qui j'en ai demandé avis ont jugé qu'il était plus expédient de faire une table à laquelle on aura recours pour trouver celles qui traitent d'une même chose.

Note to the Reader[1]
(1665)

Here is a portrait of the heart of man, which I give to the public under the name of *Moral Reflections or Moral Maxims*. It takes the chance of not pleasing everybody, because one will find perhaps that it is too faithful, and that it is not flattering enough. There are indications that the intention of the painter has never been to allow this work to appear, and that it would still be locked up in his study if a bad copy of it, which has circulated, and which has even spent some time in Holland, had not compelled one of his friends to give me another one, which he says completely conforms to the original; but, however correct it may be, it is possible that it will not avoid the censure of certain people, who cannot bear it when one takes it upon himself to penetrate to the bottom of their hearts, and who believe they have the right to prevent others from knowing them because they do not want to know themselves.

It is true that, as these *Maxims* are filled with those sorts of truths to which human pride is unable to accommodate itself, it is almost impossible that pride should not rise against them, and that they would not attract censors to themselves. Thus, it is for them that I place a *Letter*[2] here which was given to me, and which has

---

1   This note was written by La Rochefoucauld in the character of a bookseller, and it served as a "Preface" to the first edition of the *Maxims*.

2   Allusion to La Chapelle-Bessé's letter which introduced the Maxims to the reader in the 1665 edition. The letter was withdrawn in the second edition.

been written since the manuscript has appeared, and at the time when everyone took it upon himself to speak his mind about it. It has seemed to me to be proper enough to respond to the principal difficulties which one can oppose to these *Reflections*, and to explain the sentiments of their author. The *Letter* suffices to make people see that what these reflections contain is nothing but the abridgment of a morality which conforms to the thoughts of several Fathers of the Church, and that he who wrote them has had many reasons to believe that he could not lose his way by following such good guides, and that he was allowed to talk about *man* as the Fathers have talked about him; but if the respect which is owed to them is not capable of holding back the resentment of the critics, if they have no scruples about condemning the opinion of these great men by condemning this book, I pray that the reader not imitate them, not let his mind be carried away with the first movement of his heart, and, if it is possible, demand that *self-love* not take part in the judgment he will make of this book. For if the reader consults *self-love*, one cannot expect that it could be favorable to these *Maxims*: since they treat *self-love* as a corrupter of reason, it will not fail to prejudice the mind against them. Therefore, it is necessary to take care that this prejudice does not justify the critics and to be persuaded that nothing is more proper to establish the truth of these *Reflections* than the ardor and the subtlety one will exhibit in order to fight them. Indeed, it will be difficult to make any man of good sense believe that these maxims are being condemned for a motive other than that of hidden interest, pride, and self-love. In a word, the best course that the reader can take is to first put it in his mind that none of these maxims concerns him in particular, and that he alone is exempted from them, even though they appear to be general. After this, I assure him that he will be the first to subscribe to them, and that he will believe that they still spare the human heart.

Here is what I had to say about this writing in general. As for the method one might have observed in it, I believe that it would have been desirable if each *maxim* had had a title of the subject of which it treats, and if they had been put in a better order; but I could not do so without upsetting entirely the order of the copy I was given; and since there are several *maxims* about the same subject matter, those whose opinions I asked have judged that it was more expedient to make an index to which one will refer in order to find those which treat of the same thing.

Withdrawn Maxims[1]

1   *L'amour-propre est l'amour de soi-même, et de toutes choses pour soi; il rend les hommes idolâtres d'eux-mêmes, et les rendrait les tyrans des autres si la fortune leur en donnait les moyens; il ne se repose jamais hors de soi, et ne s'arrête dans les sujets étrangers que comme les abeilles sur les fleurs, pour en tirer ce qui lui est propre. Rien n'est si impétueux que ses désirs, rien de si caché que ses desseins, rien de si habile que ses conduites; ses souplesses ne se peuvent représenter, ses transformations passent celles des métamorphoses, et ses raffinements ceux de la chimie. On ne peut sonder la profondeur, ni percer les ténèbres de ses abîmes. Là il est à couvert des yeux les plus pénétrants; il y fait mille insensibles tours et retours. Là il est souvent invisible à lui-même, il y conçoit, il y nourrit, et il y élève, sans le savoir, un grand nombre d'affections et de haines; il en forme de si monstrueuses que, lorsqu'il les a mises au jour, il les méconnaît, ou il ne peut se résoudre à les avouer. De cette nuit qui le couvre naissent les ridicules persuasions qu'il a de lui-même; de là viennent ses erreurs, ses ignorances, ses grossièretés et ses niaiseries sur son sujet; de là vient qu'il croit que ses sentiments sont morts lorsqu'ils ne sont qu'endormis, qu'il s'imagine n'avoir plus envie de courir dès qu'il se repose, et qu'il pense avoir perdu tous les goûts qu'il a rassasiés. Mais cette obscurité épaisse, qui le cache à lui-même, n'empêche pas qu'il ne voie parfaitement ce qui est hors de lui, en quoi il est semblable à nos yeux, qui découvrent tout, et sont aveugles seulement pour eux-mêmes. En effet dans ses plus*

1   La Rochefoucauld withdrew these maxims from earlier editions of the work.

101

grands intérêts, et dans ses plus importantes affaires, où la violence de ses souhaits appelle toute son attention, il voit, il sent, il entend, il imagine, il soupçonne, il pénètre, il devine tout; de sorte qu'on est tenté de croire que chacune de ses passions a une espèce de magie qui lui est propre. Rien n'est si intime et si fort que ses attachements, qu'il essaye de rompre inutilement à la vue des malheurs extrêmes qui le menacent. Cependant il fait quelquefois en peu de temps, et sans aucun effort, ce qu'il n'a pu faire avec tous ceux dont il est capable dans le cours de plusieurs années; d'où l'on pourrait conclure assez vraisemblablement que c'est par lui-même que ses désirs sont allumés, plutôt que par la beauté et par le mérite de ses objets; que son goût est le prix qui les relève, et le fard qui les embellit; que c'est après lui-même qu'il court, et qu'il suit son gré, lorsqu'il suit les choses qui sont à son gré. Il est tous les contraires: il est impérieux et obéissant, sincère et dissimulé, miséricordieux et cruel, timide et audacieux. Il a de différentes inclinations selon la diversité des tempéraments qui le tournent, et le dévouent tantôt à la gloire, tantôt aux richesses, et tantôt aux plaisirs; il en change selon le changement de nos âges, de nos fortunes et de nos expériences; mais il lui est indifférent d'en avoir plusieurs ou de n'en avoir qu'une, parce qu'il se partage en plusieurs et se ramasse en une quand il le faut, et comme il lui plaît. Il est inconstant, et outre les changements qui viennent des causes étrangères, il y en a une infinité qui naissent de lui, et de son propre fonds; il est inconstant d'inconstance, de légèreté, d'amour, de nouveauté, de lassitude et de dégoût; il est capricieux, et on le voit quelquefois travailler avec le dernier empressement, et avec des travaux incroyables, à obtenir des choses qui ne lui sont point avantageuses, et qui même lui sont nuisibles, mais qu'il poursuit parce qu'il les veut. Il est bizarre, et met souvent toute son application dans les emplois les plus frivoles; il trouve tout son plaisir dans les plus fades, et conserve toute sa fierté dans les plus méprisables. Il est dans tous les états de la vie, et dans toutes les conditions; il vit partout, et il vit de tout, il vit de rien; il s'accommode des choses, et de leur privation; il passe même dans le parti des gens

qui lui font la guerre, il entre dans leurs desseins; et ce qui est
admirable, il se hait lui-même avec eux, il conjure sa perte, il tra-
vaille même à sa ruine. Enfin il ne se soucie que d'être, et pourvu qu'il
soit, il veut bien être son ennemi. Il ne faut donc pas s'étonner s'il se
joint quelquefois à la plus rude austérité, et s'il entre si hardiment en
société avec elle pour se détruire, parce que, dans le même temps qu'il
se ruine en un endroit, il se rétablit en un autre; quand on pense qu'il
quitte son plaisir, il ne fait que le suspendre, ou le changer, et lors même
qu'il est vaincu et qu'on croit en être défait, on le retrouve qui triom-
phe dans sa propre défaite. Voilà la peinture de l'amour-propre, dont
toute la vie n'est qu'une grande et longue agitation; la mer en est une
image sensible, et l'amour-propre trouve dans le flux et le reflux de ses
vagues continuelles une fidèle expression de la succession turbulente de
ses pensées, et de ses éternels mouvements.

1   Self-love is the love of oneself, and of all things for oneself; it
renders men idolatrous of themselves, and would render them
tyrants of others if fortune gave them the means to do so; it
never rests outside of itself, and only settles on things foreign to
it, like bees on flowers, to draw from them what is proper to it.
Nothing is as impetuous as its desires, nothing as hidden as its
designs, nothing as clever as the things it does; its suppleness
cannot be represented, its transformations surpass those of
metamorphosis, and its refinements those of chemistry. One
cannot probe its depth, nor pierce the darkness of its abyss.
There it is hidden from the most penetrating eyes; it makes a
thousand imperceptible twists and turns. There it is often invisible to itself; there it conceives, there it nourishes, and there it
raises – without knowing it – a great number of affections and
hatreds; there it forms some that are so monstrous that, when it
brings them into the light, it fails to recognize them as its own,
or it cannot bring itself to acknowledge them as its own. From
the night which covers it, the ridiculous convictions which it has
about itself are born; from this comes its errors, its ignorance,

its rudeness, and its silliness about itself; from this comes its belief that its sentiments are dead when they are merely dormant. It imagines that it no longer desires to run as soon as it rests, and it thinks it has lost whatever tastes it has satisfied. But this thick obscurity, which hides it from itself, does not prevent it from seeing clearly what is outside itself; in this regard it is similar to our eyes, which discover everything, and are blind only to themselves. Indeed, in the greatest matters of self-interest, and in its most important affairs, where the violence of its wishes calls for its complete attention, it sees, it feels, it hears, it imagines, it suspects, it penetrates, it divines everything – so that one is tempted to believe that each of its passions has a kind of magic which is proper to it. Nothing is so intimate and so strong as the bonds of affection that it tries uselessly to break at the sight of the extreme misfortunes that threaten it. However, it sometimes does, in little time, and without any effort, what it was unable to do with all of the efforts of which it is capable in the course of several years. From this one could conclude, with some likelihood, that it is through itself that its desires are alighted, rather than from the beauty and worth of its objects; that its taste is the measure which seasons them, and the make-up which adorns them; that it is after itself that it runs, and that it follows its pleasure, when it follows the things that are according to its pleasure. It is all the contraries: it is imperious and obedient, sincere and dissimulating, merciful and cruel, timid and audacious. It has some different inclinations depending upon the diversity of the temperaments which direct it, and which are dedicated now to glory, now to riches, and now to pleasures; it changes these inclinations according to the changes in our age, our fortunes, and our experiences; but it makes no difference to it whether it has several or only one inclination, because it becomes many and gathers itself into one when necessary, as it pleases. It is inconstant, and besides the changes that come from causes foreign to it, there is an infinite number that are born from it, and from its own stock; it is inconstant of inconstancy, of light-mindedness, of love, of novelty, of weariness, and of disgust. It is capricious, and one sees it sometimes work with the greatest alacrity, and with incredible labor to obtain things that are not advantageous to it, and that are even harmful to it, but which it pursues because it wants them. It is bizarre, and often places all of its diligence into the most frivolous occupations; it finds all its pleasure in the most insipid ones, and maintains all of its pride in the most despicable. It is in every state of life, and in every condition; it lives everywhere; it lives off everything, it lives off nothing; it accommodates itself to things and to their privation. It enlists even in the party of those who wage war against it; it enters into their designs; and, what is admirable, it hates itself with them; it plots its own fall; it even works toward its own ruin. Finally, it concerns itself only about being, and as long as it is, it consents to being its own enemy. One must therefore not be surprised that it is sometimes joined to the severest austerity, and if it enters so boldly into society with this austerity in order to destroy itself, because at the same time that it ruins itself in one place, it reestablishes itself in another. When one thinks that it leaves its pleasure behind, it is only delaying it, or changing it; and even though it is vanquished and one believes oneself rid of it, one finds it again, victorious in its own defeat. Here is the portrait of self-love, whose whole life is only a great and long agitation. The sea is a fitting image of it, and self-love finds in the ebb and flow of its continual waves a faithful expression of the turbulent succession of its thoughts, and of its eternal movements.

2   *Toutes les passions ne sont autre chose que les divers degrés de la chaleur, et de la froideur, du sang.*

2   All the passions are nothing but the diverse degrees of the warmth and coldness of the blood.

3   *La modération dans la bonne fortune n'est que l'appréhension de la honte qui suit l'emportement, ou la peur de perdre ce que l'on a.*
Moderation in good fortune is only the apprehension of the shame which results from fits of anger, or the fear of losing what one has.

4   *La modération est comme la sobriété: on voudrait bien manger davantage, mais on craint de se faire mal.*
Moderation is like sobriety: one would love to eat more, but one fears hurting oneself.

5   *Tout le monde trouve à redire en autrui ce qu'on trouve à redire en lui.*
Everyone criticizes in others the fault that others criticize in him.

6   *L'orgueil, comme lassé de ses artifices et de ses différentes métamorphoses, après avoir joué tout seul tous les personnages de la comédie humaine, se montre avec un visage naturel, et se découvre par la fierté; de sorte qu'à proprement parler la fierté est l'éclat et la déclaration de l'orgueil.*
Pride, as if weary of its artifices and of its different metamorphoses, after having played all alone all of the characters of the human comedy, shows itself with a natural face, and reveals itself through haughtiness; so that properly speaking, haughtiness is the dazzling affirmation of pride.

7   *La complexion qui fait le talent pour les petites choses est contraire à celle qu'il faut pour le talent des grandes.*

7 The temperament that makes the talent for small things is contrary to the one needed for the talent for great ones.

8 *C'est une espèce de bonheur, de connaître jusques à quel point on doit être malheureux.*
It is a kind of happiness to know up to what point one has to be unhappy.

9 *On n'est jamais si malheureux qu'on croit, ni si heureux qu'on avait espéré.*
One is never as unhappy as one believes, nor as happy as one had hoped.

10 *On se console souvent d'être malheureux par un certain plaisir qu'on trouve à le paraître.*
One often consoles oneself for being unhappy through a certain pleasure one finds in appearing to be so.

11 *Il faudrait pouvoir répondre de sa fortune, pour pouvoir répondre de ce que l'on fera.*
One would have to be able to answer for one's fortune, to be able to answer for what one will do.

12 *Comment peut-on répondre de ce qu'on voudra à l'avenir, puisque l'on ne sait pas précisément ce que l'on veut dans le temps présent?*
How can one answer for what one will want in the future, since one does not know precisely what one wants in the present?

13 *L'amour est à l'âme de celui qui aime ce qui l'âme est au corps qu'elle anime.*
Love is to the soul of him who loves what the soul is to the body that it animates.

14 *La justice n'est qu'une vive appréhension qu'on ne nous ôte ce qui nous appartient; de là vient cette considération et ce respect pour tous les intérêts du prochain, et cette scrupuleuse application à ne lui faire aucun préjudice; cette crainte retient l'homme dans les bornes des biens que la naissance, ou la fortune, lui ont donnés, et sans cette crainte il ferait des courses continuelles sur les autres.*

Justice is only a vivid fear that another will take away what belongs to us; from this comes the consideration and the respect for all of the interests of our fellow beings, and the scrupulous care to do them no harm; this fear restrains man within the limits of the goods which birth, or fortune, have given him, and without this fear he would make continual attacks against others.

15 *La justice, dans les juges qui sont modérés, n'est que l'amour de leur élévation.*

Justice, in judges who are moderate, is only the love of their eminence.

16 *On blâme l'injustice, non pas par l'aversion que l'on a pour elle, mais pour le préjudice que l'on en reçoit.*

Injustice is blamed, not out of aversion, but because of the harm it does.

17 *Le premier mouvement de joie que nous avons du bonheur de nos amis ne vient ni de la bonté de notre naturel, ni de l'amitié que nous avons pour eux; c'est un effet de l'amour-propre qui nous flatte de l'espérance d'être heureux à notre tour, ou de retirer quelque utilité de leur bonne fortune.*

The first movement of joy which we come to have from the happiness of our friends comes neither from the goodness of our nature, nor from the friendship we have for them; it is an effect of self-love which flatters us with the hope of being happy in our turn, or of drawing something useful out of their good fortune.

18 *Dans l'adversité de nos meilleurs amis, nous trouvons toujours quelque chose qui ne nous déplaît pas.*
Amidst the adversity of our best friends, we always find something which does not displease us.

19 *L'aveuglement des hommes est le plus dangereux effet de leur orgueil: il sert à le nourrir et à l'augmenter, et nous ôte la connaissance des remèdes qui pourraient soulager nos misères et nous guérir de nos défauts.*
The blindness of men is the most dangerous result of their pride: it helps to nourish it and to increase it, and deprives us of the knowledge of the remedies which could relieve our miseries and cure us of our shortcomings.

20 *On n'a plus de raison, quand on n'espère plus d'en trouver aux autres.*
One no longer has any reason, when one no longer hopes to find some in others.

21 *Les philosophes, et Sénèque surtout, n'ont point ôté les crimes par leurs préceptes: ils n'ont fait que les employer au bâtiment de l'orgueil.*
The philosophers, and Seneca above all, have not eliminated crimes with their precepts: they have only employed them for the building of pride.

22 *Les plus sages le sont dans les choses indifférentes, mais ils ne le sont presque jamais dans leurs plus sérieuses affaires.*
The wisest are wise in unimportant things, but they are almost never wise in their most serious affairs.

23 *La plus subtile folie est faite de la plus subtile sagesse.*
The subtlest folly is made of the subtlest wisdom.

24 *La sobriété est l'amour de la santé, ou l'impuissance de manger beaucoup.*
Sobriety is the love of health, or the inability of eating a lot.

25 *Chaque talent dans les hommes, de même que chaque arbre, a ses propriétés et ses effets qui lui sont tous particuliers.*
Every talent in men, as well as every tree, has its properties and its effects, every one of which is particular to it.

26 *On n'oublie jamais mieux les choses que quand on s'est lassé d'en parler.*
One never forgets things better than when one has tired of talking about them.

27 *La modestie, qui semble refuser les louanges, n'est en effet qu'un désir d'en avoir de plus délicates.*
Modesty, which seems to refuse praises, is in fact only a desire for more subtle praise.

28 *On ne blâme le vice et on ne loue la vertu que par intérêt.*
One only blames vice and one only praises virtue out of self-interest.

29 *L'amour-propre empêche bien que celui qui nous flatte ne soit jamais celui qui nous flatte le plus.*
Self-love indeed prevents the case that he who flatters us never is he who flatters us most.

30 *On ne fait point de distinction dans les espèces de colères, bien qu'il y en ait une légère et quasi innocente, qui vient de l'ardeur de la com-*

*plexion, et une autre très criminelle, qui est à proprement parler la
fureur de l'orgueil.*

One does not make any distinction between the kinds of anger,
even though there is one light and quasi-innocent, which comes
from the ardor of the temperament, and another one, most
criminal, which is properly speaking, the furor of pride.

31 *Les grandes âmes ne sont pas celles qui ont moins de passions et plus
de vertu que les âmes communes, mais celles seulement qui ont de plus
grands desseins.*

The great souls are not those who have fewer passions and more
virtues than the common souls, but only those who have greater
designs.

32 *La férocité naturelle fait moins de cruels que l'amour-propre.*

Natural ferocity makes fewer people cruel than self-love.

33 *On peut dire de toutes nos vertus ce qu'un poète italien a dit de l'honnêteté des femmes, que ce n'est souvent autre chose qu'un art de
paraître honnête.*

One can say about all of our virtues what an Italian poet[2] said
about the honesty of women, that it is often nothing but an art
to appear honest.

34 *Ce que le monde nomme vertu n'est d'ordinaire qu'un fantôme formé
par nos passions, à qui on donne un nom honnête, pour faire impunément ce qu'on veut.*

What the world calls virtue is ordinarily only a phantom formed
by our passions, to which one gives an honest name, in order to
do with impunity what one wants.

2   La Rochefoucauld has in mind a passage of Act III, scene 5, of Guarini's
Pastor Fido: "Ch'altro al fin l'honestate / No è, che un' arte di parere honesta."
[For what in the end is honesty / but an art to appear honest.]

35 *Nous n'avouons jamais nos défauts que par vanité.*
We never confess our faults but out of vanity.

36 *On ne trouve point dans l'homme le bien ni le mal dans l'excès.*
One does not find in man good or evil in excess.

37 *Ceux qui sont incapables de commettre de grands crimes n'en soupçon-*
nent pas facilement les autres.
Those who are incapable of committing great crimes do not easily suspect others of them.

38 *La pompe des enterrements regarde plus la vanité des vivants que*
l'honneur des morts.
The pomp of burials concerns the vanity of the living more than
the honor of the dead.

39 *Quelque incertitude et quelque variété qui paraisse dans le monde, on*
y remarque néanmoins un certain enchaînement secret, et un ordre
réglé de tout temps par la Providence, qui fait que chaque chose
marche en son rang, et suit le cours de sa destinée.
Whatever uncertainty and whatever variety appear in the world,
one nonetheless notes in it a certain secret succession, and an
order regulated at all times by Providence, which causes each
thing to proceed within its proper order, and follows the course
of its destiny.

40 *L'intrépidité doit soutenir le cœur dans les conjurations, au lieu que la*
seule valeur lui fournit toute la fermeté qui lui est nécessaire dans les
périls de la guerre.
Intrepidity has to sustain the heart in conspiracies, whereas
valor alone furnishes it with all the firmness which is necessary
to it in the perils of war.

41 *Ceux qui voudraient définir la victoire par sa naissance seraient ten-*
tés comme les poètes de l'appeler la fille du Ciel, puisqu'on ne trouve
point son origine sur la terre. En effet elle est produite par infinité
d'actions qui, au lieu de l'avoir pour but, regardent seulement les
intérêts particuliers de ceux qui les font, puisque tous ceux qui com-
posent une armée, allant à leur propre gloire et à leur élévation, pro-
curent un bien si grand et si général.

Those who would want to define victory by its birth would be
tempted like the poets to call it the daughter of Heaven, since
one does not find its origin upon the earth. Indeed it is produced by an infinite number of actions which, instead of having
it as a goal, consider only the particular interests of those who
do them, since all those who compose an army, aiming at their
own glory and elevation, procure so great and so general a good.

42 *On ne peut répondre de son courage quand on n'a jamais été dans le*
péril.

One cannot answer for one's courage when one has never been
in peril.

43 *L'imitation est toujours malheureuse, et tout ce qui est contrefait*
déplaît avec les mêmes choses qui charment lorsqu'elles sont naturelles.

Imitation is always unfortunate, and all that is counterfeited
displeases with the very things which charm when they are natural.

44 *Il est bien malaisé de distinguer la bonté générale, et répandue sur tout*
le monde, de la grande habileté.

It is quite difficult to distinguish the goodness – general and
found in everyone – from great cleverness.[3]

3   This maxim admits of another translation: "It is quite difficult to distinguish
between that goodness which applies itself to everyone and great cleverness."

45 *Pour pouvoir être toujours bon, il faut que les autres croient qu'ils ne peuvent jamais nous être impunément méchants.*
In order to be always good, it is necessary that others believe that they never can be mean to us with impunity.

46 *La confiance de plaire est souvent un moyen de déplaire infailliblement.*
The confidence to please is often a means to displease infallibly.

47 *La confiance que l'on a en soi fait naître la plus grande partie de celle que l'on a aux autres.*
The confidence one has in oneself gives birth to the greater part of the confidence one has in others.

48 *Il y a une révolution générale qui change le goût des esprits, aussi bien que les fortunes du monde.*
There is a general movement which changes intellectual tastes, as well as the fortunes of the world.

49 *La vérité est le fondement et la raison de la perfection, et de la beauté; une chose, de quelque nature qu'elle soit, ne saurait être belle, et parfaite, si elle n'est véritablement tout ce qu'elle doit être, et si elle n'a tout ce qu'elle doit avoir.*
Truth is the foundation and the ground of perfection, and of beauty; a thing, whatever its nature may be, cannot be beautiful, and perfect, if it is not truly all that it can be, and if it does not have all that it must have.

50 *Il y a de belles choses qui ont plus d'éclat quand elles demeurent imparfaites que quand elles sont trop achevées.*
There are fine things which are more dazzling when they remain imperfect than when they are too accomplished.

51 *La magnanimité est un noble effort de l'orgueil par lequel il rend l'homme maître de lui-même pour le rendre maître de toutes choses.*
Magnanimity is a noble effort of pride which makes man master of himself in order to make him master of all things.

52 *Le luxe et la trop grande politesse dans les États sont le présage assuré de leur décadence parce que, tous les particuliers s'attachant à leurs intérêts propres, ils se détournent du bien public.*
Luxury and too great a politeness in the Estates are the portent of their decadence because, all individuals being fond of their own interests, they turn away from the public good.

53 *Rien ne prouve tant que les philosophes ne sont pas si persuadés qu'ils disent que la mort n'est pas un mal, que le tourment qu'ils se donnent pour établir l'immortalité de leur nom par la perte de la vie.*
Nothing proves as well that philosophers are not as convinced as they claim that death is not an evil, as the torment they go through in order to establish the immortality of their names by the loss of their lives.

54 *De toutes les passions celle qui est la plus inconnue à nous-mêmes, c'est la paresse; elle est la plus ardente et la plus maligne de toutes, quoique sa violence soit insensible, et que les dommages qu'elle cause soient très cachés; si nous considérons attentivement son pouvoir, nous verrons qu'elle se rend en toutes rencontres maîtresse de nos sentiments, de nos intérêts et de nos plaisirs; c'est la rémore qui a la force d'arrêter les plus grands vaisseaux, c'est une bonace plus dangereuse aux plus importantes affaires que les écueils, et que les plus grandes tempêtes; le repos de la paresse est un charme secret de l'âme qui suspend soudainement les plus ardentes poursuites et les plus opiniâtres résolutions; pour donner enfin la véritable idée de cette passion, il faut dire que la paresse est comme une béatitude de l'âme, qui la console de toutes ses pertes, et qui lui tient lieu de tous les biens.*

54 Of all the passions the one which is most unknown to ourselves
is laziness; it is the most ardent and the most malignant of all,
although its violence is insensible, and the damage it causes is
quite hidden; if we attentively consider its power, we will see
that on every occasion it makes itself master of our sentiments,
our interests, and our pleasures; it is the remora[4] which has the
strength to stop the greatest ships, it is a lull more dangerous to
the most important matters than reefs and the greatest storms;
the repose of laziness is a secret charm of the soul which suddenly suspends the most ardent pursuits and the most obstinate
resolutions; in order finally to give the true idea of this passion,
it is necessary to say that laziness is like a beatitude of the soul,
which consoles it for all of its losses, and which takes the place
of every good.

55 *Il est plus facile de prendre de l'amour quand on n'en a pas, que de
s'en défaire quand on en a.*
It is easier to take some love when one does not have any, than
to rid oneself of it when one has some.

56 *La plupart des femmes se rendent plutôt par faiblesse que par passion;
de là vient que pour l'ordinaire les hommes entreprenants réussissent
mieux que les autres, quoiqu'ils ne soient pas plus aimables.*
Most women surrender out of weakness rather than out of passion; from this it follows that ordinarily, enterprising men succeed better than the others, even though they are not more amiable.

57 *N'aimer guère en amour est un moyen assuré pour être aimé.*
In love, to love very little is a sure means to be loved.

4   Small fish, common in the Mediterranean, which attach themselves to bigger
fish or to boats. La Rochefoucauld is alluding to the legend according to
which their peculiarity enables them to bring boats to a stop.

58 *La sincérité que se demandent les amants et les maîtresses, pour savoir l'un et l'autre quand ils cesseront de s'aimer, est bien moins pour vouloir être avertis quand on ne les aimera plus que pour être mieux assurés qu'on les aime lorsque l'on ne dit point le contraire.*

The sincerity which lovers and mistresses ask of each other for them to know when they cease to love, is much less because they want to be warned when they will not be loved anymore, than in order to be more reassured that they are loved when the other does not say the contrary.

59 *La plus juste comparaison qu'on puisse faire de l'amour, c'est celle de la fièvre; nous n'avons non plus de pouvoir sur l'un que sur l'autre, soit pour sa violence ou pour sa durée.*

The most just comparison that one may make of love is to fever; we do not have power over one any more than the other, whether for its violence or its duration.

60 *La plus grande habileté des moins habiles est de se savoir soumettre à la bonne conduite d'autrui.*

The greatest cleverness of the least clever is knowing how to submit to the proper guidance of others.

61 *Quand on ne trouve pas son repos en soi-même, il est inutile de le chercher ailleurs.*

When one does not find one's repose in oneself, it is useless to look for it elsewhere.

62 *Comme on n'est jamais en liberté d'aimer, ou de cesser d'aimer, l'a-mant ne peut se plaindre avec justice de l'inconstance de sa maîtresse, ni elle de la légèreté de son amant.*

Since one is never at liberty to love, or to cease to love, the lover can never complain with justice of the inconstancy of his mistress, nor she of the frivolity of her lover.

63 *Quand nous sommes las d'aimer, nous sommes bien aises qu'on nous devienne infidèle, pour nous dégager de notre fidélité.*
When we are weary of loving, we are quite pleased that the other has become unfaithful to us, so that we may be released from our faithfulness.

64 *Comment prétendons-nous qu'un autre garde notre secret si nous ne pouvons le garder nous-mêmes?*
How can we expect another to keep our secret if we cannot keep it ourselves?

65 *Il n'y en a point qui pressent tant les autres que les paresseux lorsqu'ils ont satisfait à leur paresse, afin de paraître diligents.*
Nobody pressures others as much as the lazy when they have satisfied their laziness in order to appear diligent.

66 *C'est une preuve de peu d'amitié de ne s'apercevoir pas du refroidissement de celle de nos amis.*
It is proof of a meager friendship not to perceive the cooling of that of our friends.

67 *Les rois font des hommes comme des pièces de monnaie; ils les font valoir ce qu'ils veulent, et l'on est forcé de les recevoir selon leur cours, et non pas selon leur véritable prix.*
Kings make men like coins; they make them cost what they want, and one is forced to take them according to their current value, and not according to their true price.

68 *Il y a des crimes qui deviennent innocents et même glorieux par leur éclat, leur nombre et leur excès. De là vient que les voleries publiques sont des habiletés, et que prendre des provinces injustement s'appelle faire des conquêtes.*
Some crimes become innocent and even glorious by being so

dazzling, numerous, and extreme. From this it follows that public swindles are clever, and that acquiring provinces unjustly is called making conquests.

69 *On donne plus aisément des bornes à sa reconnaissance qu'à ses espérances et qu'à ses désirs.*
One more easily gives limits to one's gratitude, than to one's hopes and one's desires.

70 *Nous ne regrettons pas toujours la perte de nos amis par la considération de leur mérite, mais par celle de nos besoins et de la bonne opinion qu'ils avaient de nous.*
We do not always regret the loss of our friends out of consideration for their merit, but out of consideration for our needs and for the good opinion they had of us.

71 *On aime à deviner les autres; mais l'on n'aime pas à être deviné.*
One likes to see through others; but one does not like to be seen through.

72 *C'est une ennuyeuse maladie que de conserver sa santé par un trop grand régime.*
It is a boring illness to keep one's health with too rigorous a diet.

73 *On craint toujours de voir ce qu'on aime, quand on vient de faire des coquetteries ailleurs.*
One always fears seeing what one loves, when one just flirted somewhere else.

74 *On doit se consoler de ses fautes, quand on a la force de les avouer.*
One should console oneself for one's faults, when one has the strength to confess them.

Posthumous Maxims[1]

1   *Comme la plus heureuse personne du monde est celle à qui peu de
    choses suffit, les grands et les ambitieux sont en ce point les plus mis-
    érables qu'il leur faut l'assemblage d'une infinité de biens pour les ren-
    dre heureux.*
    Just as the happiest person in the world is the one for whom few
    things suffice, the great and the ambitious are in this regard the
    most miserable to the extent that they need the combination of
    an infinity of goods in order to make them happy.

2   *La finesse n'est qu'une pauvre habileté.*
    Shrewdness is only a poor cleverness.

3   *Les philosophes ne condamnent les richesses que par le mauvais usage
    que nous en faisons; il dépend de nous de les acquérir et de nous en
    servir sans crime et, au lieu qu'elles nourrissent et accroissent les vices,
    comme le bois entretient et augmente le feu, nous pouvons les con-
    sacrer à toutes les vertus et les rendre même par là plus agréables et
    plus éclatantes.*
    Philosophers only condemn riches through the bad use that we
    make of them; it depends on us to acquire them and to use them

---

1   These maxims are from a variety of manuscript sources, and although a few
    appeared in print, La Rochefoucauld himself never offered them for publica-
    tion. They have, however, traditionally been collected and published in edi-
    tions of his writings.

without crime, and, instead of their nourishing and increasing vices, as wood keeps and increases fire, we can consecrate them to all of the virtues and even render them in this way more agreeable and more dazzling.

4 *La ruine du prochain plaît aux amis et aux ennemis.*
   The ruin of a neighbor pleases friends and enemies.

5 *Chacun pense être plus fin que les autres.*
   Each thinks he is shrewder than the others.

6 *On ne saurait compter toutes les espèces de vanité.*
   One cannot count all of the kinds of vanity.

7 *Ce qui nous empêche souvent de bien juger des sentences qui prouvent la fausseté des vertus, c'est que nous croyons trop aisément qu'elles sont véritables en nous.*
   What often prevents us from weighing well the judgments which prove the falsity of virtues is that we believe too easily that they are true in us.

8 *Nous craignons toutes choses comme mortels, et nous désirons toutes choses comme si nous étions immortels.*
   We fear all things as mortals, and we desire all things as if we were immortal.

9 *Dieu a mis des talents différents dans l'homme comme il a planté de différents arbres dans la nature, en sorte que chaque talent de même que chaque arbre a ses propriétés et ses effets qui lui sont tous particuliers; de là vient que le poirier le meilleur du monde ne saurait porter les pommes les plus communes, et que le talent le plus excellent ne saurait produire les mêmes effets des talents les plus communs; de là vient encore qu'il est aussi ridicule de vouloir faire des sentences sans*

en avoir la graine en soi que de vouloir qu'un parterre produise des
tulipes quoiqu'on n'y ait point semé les oignons.

God has put different talents in man as he has planted different
trees in nature, so that each talent as well as each tree has its
properties and its effects, each of which are particular to it; from
this it follows that the best pear tree in the world could not bear
the most common apples, and that the most excellent talent
could not produce the same effects as the most common talents;
from this it also follows that it is as ridiculous to want to make
judgments without having the seed of them in oneself as want-
ing a flower-bed to produce tulips even though one has not
sown any bulbs in it.

10 *Une preuve convaincante que l'homme n'a pas été créé comme il est,*
    c'est que plus il devient raisonnable et plus il rougit en soi-même de
    l'extravagance, de la bassesse et de la corruption de ses sentiments et
    de ses inclinations.

    A convincing proof that man has not been created as he is, is
    that the more he becomes reasonable, the more he blushes with-
    in himself from the extravagance, from the baseness and from
    the corruption of his sentiments and of his inclinations.

11 *Il ne faut pas s'offenser que les autres nous cachent la vérité puisque*
    nous nous la cachons si souvent nous-mêmes.

    We must not take offense that others hide the truth from us,
    since we ourselves hide it so often from ourselves.

12 *Rien ne prouve davantage combien la mort est redoutable que la peine*
    que les philosophes se donnent pour persuader qu'on la doit mépriser.

    Nothing proves more how dreadful death is than the trouble
    philosophers take in order to persuade that one ought to despise
    it.

13 *Il semble que c'est le diable qui a tout exprès placé la paresse sur la frontière de plusieurs vertus.*
It seems that it is the devil who has entirely on purpose placed laziness on the border of several virtues.

14 *La fin du bien est un mal; la fin du mal est un bien.*
The end of good is an evil; the end of evil is a good.

15 *On blâme aisément les défauts des autres, mais on s'en sert rarement à corriger les siens.*
One easily blames the shortcomings of others, but one rarely uses them in order to correct one's own.

16 *Les biens et les maux qui nous arrivent ne nous touchent pas selon leur grandeur, mais selon notre sensibilité.*
The good and evil which happen to us do not touch us according to their greatness but according to our sensibility.

17 *Ceux qui prisent trop leur noblesse ne prisent d'ordinaire pas assez ce qui en est l'origine.*
Those who value their nobility too much do not ordinarily value enough what its origin is.

18 *Le remède de la jalousie est la certitude de ce qu'on craint, parce qu'elle cause la fin de la vie ou la fin de l'amour; c'est un cruel remède, mais il est plus doux que les doutes et les soupçons.*
The remedy of jealousy is the certainty of what we fear, because it causes the end of life or the end of love; it is a cruel remedy, but it is sweeter than doubts and suspicions.

19 *Il est difficile de comprendre combien est grande la ressemblance et la différence qu'il y a entre tous les hommes.*

19 It is difficult to understand how great are the resemblances and the differences that there are among all men.

20 *Ce qui fait tant disputer contre les maximes qui découvrent le cœur de l'homme, c'est que l'on craint d'y être découvert.*
What makes one argue so much against the maxims which uncover the heart of man is that one fears being discovered in them.

21 *L'homme est si misérable que, tournant toutes ses conduites à satisfaire ses passions, il gémit incessamment sous leur tyrannie; il ne peut supporter ni leur violence ni celle qu'il faut qu'il se fasse pour s'affranchir de leur joug; il trouve du dégoût non seulement dans ses vices, mais encore dans leurs remèdes, et ne peut s'accommoder ni des chagrins de ses maladies ni du travail de sa guérison.*
Man is so miserable that, directing all of his conduct to satisfy his passions, he ceaselessly moans under their tyranny; he can neither bear their violence nor the violence he must do to himself in order to free himself from their yoke; he finds disgust not only in his vices, but also in their remedies, and can neither accommodate himself with the sorrows of his maladies nor with the work of his cure.

22 *Dieu a permis, pour punir l'homme du péché originel, qu'il se fît un dieu de son amour-propre pour en être tourmenté dans toutes les actions de sa vie.*
God has allowed, in order to punish man for original sin, that man make a god of his self-love in order to be tormented by it in all of the actions of his life.

23 *L'espérance et la crainte sont inséparables, et il n'y a point de crainte sans espérance ni d'espérance sans crainte.*

23 Hope and fear are inseparable, and there is no fear without hope nor hope without fear.

24 *Le pouvoir que les personnes que nous aimons ont sur nous est presque toujours plus grand que celui que nous y avons nous-mêmes.*
The power that the people we love have over us is almost always greater that the one we ourselves have.

25 *Ce qui nous fait croire si facilement que les autres ont des défauts, c'est la facilité que l'on a de croire ce qu'on souhaite.*
What makes us believe so easily that others have shortcomings is the ease of believing what one wishes.

26 *L'intérêt est l'âme de l'amour-propre, de sorte que, comme le corps, privé de son âme, est sans vue, sans ouïe, sans connaissance, sans sentiment et sans mouvement, de même, l'amour-propre séparé, s'il le faut dire ainsi, de son intérêt, ne voit, n'entend, ne sent et ne se remue plus; de là vient qu'un même homme qui court la terre et les mers pour son intérêt devient soudainement paralytique pour l'intérêt des autres; de là vient le soudain assoupissement et cette mort que nous causons à tous ceux à qui nous contons nos affaires; de là vient leur prompte résurrection lorsque dans notre narration nous y mêlons quelque chose qui les regarde; de sorte que nous voyons dans nos conversations et dans nos traités que dans un même moment un homme perd connaissance et revient à soi, selon que son propre intérêt s'approche de lui ou qu'il s'en retire.*
Self-interest is the soul of self-love, so that just as the body deprived of its soul is without sight, without hearing, without consciousness, without sentiment and without movement, so self-love deprived – if it must thus be said – of its self-interest does not see, does not hear, does not feel, and does not move itself anymore; from this it follows that the same man who

roams the earth and seas for his self-interest suddenly becomes paralyzed for the interest of others; from this comes the sudden slumber and the death which we cause in those to whom we tell about our affairs; from this comes their prompt resurrection when we put in our narration something which pertains to them; so that we see in our conversations and in our negotiations that at the same moment a man loses consciousness or comes back to himself, depending on whether his own self-interest comes closer to him or withdraws from him.

27 *On ne donne des louanges que pour en profiter.*
One gives away praises only to profit from them.

28 *Les passions ne sont que les divers goûts de l'amour-propre.*
Passions are only the diverse tastes of self-love.

29 *L'extrême ennui sert à nous désennuyer.*
Extreme *ennui* serves to take *ennui* away from us.

30 *On loue et on blâme la plupart des choses parce que c'est la mode de les louer ou de les blâmer.*
One praises and blames most things because it is in fashion to praise them or to blame them.

31 *Il n'est jamais plus difficile de bien parler que lorsqu'on ne parle que de peur de se taire.*
It is never more difficult to speak well than when one speaks only out of fear of not speaking.

32 *Si on avait ôté à ce qu'on appelle force le désir de conserver, et la crainte de perdre, il ne lui resterait pas grand'chose.*
If one had taken away from what one calls strength the desire to preserve and the fear of losing, not much would remain to it.

33 *La familiarité est un relâchement presque de toutes les règles de la vie civile, que le libertinage a introduit dans la société pour nous faire parvenir à celle qu'on appelle commode. C'est un effet de l'amour-propre qui, voulant tout accommoder à notre faiblesse, nous soustrait à l'honnête sujétion que nous imposent les bonnes mœurs et, pour chercher trop les moyens de nous les rendre commodes, les fait dégénérer en vices. Les femmes, ayant naturellement plus de mollesse que les hommes, tombent plutôt dans ce relâchement, et y perdent davantage: l'autorité du sexe ne se maintient pas, le respect qu'on lui doit diminue, et l'on peut dire que l'honnête y perd la plus grande partie de ses droits.*

Familiarity is a neglect of almost all of the rules of civil life, which libertinage has introduced into society in order to make us achieve the life one calls convenient. It is an effect of self-love which, being willing to accommodate everything to our weakness, draws us away from the honest subjection that good mores impose on us and seeking too much the means to render mores convenient to us, makes them degenerate into vices. Women, naturally being softer than men, fall sooner into this neglect, and lose more in it: the authority of the sex does not maintain itself, the respect one owes to it diminishes, and one can say that proper conduct loses the greatest part of its rights there.

34 *La raillerie est une gaieté agréable de l'esprit, qui enjoue la conversation, et qui lie la société si elle est obligeante, ou qui la trouble si elle ne l'est pas. Elle est plus pour celui qui la fait que pour celui qui la souffre. C'est toujours un combat de bel esprit, que produit la vanité; d'où vient que ceux qui en manquent pour la soutenir, et ceux qu'un défaut reproché fait rougir, s'en offense également, comme d'une défaite injurieuse qu'ils ne sauraient pardonner. C'est un poison qui tout pur éteint l'amitié et excite la haine, mais qui corrigé par l'agrément de l'esprit, et la flatterie de la louange, l'acquiert ou la conserve; et il en faut user sobrement avec ses amis et avec les faibles.*

34 Raillery is an agreeable gaiety of the mind that makes conversation pleasant and binds society when it is obliging, or which troubles it when it is not. It is more for him who says it than for him who bears it. It is always a fight of sharp wits that vanity produces; from this it follows that those who lack the wit to sustain it, and those who blush when being reproached for a shortcoming, equally take offense from it, as from an insulting defeat which they cannot forgive. It is a poison which, when entirely pure, extinguishes friendship and excites hatred, but which, when corrected by the agreement of wit and the flattery of praise, acquires friendship or preserves it; and one must use it soberly with one's friends and with the weak.

35 *Force gens veulent être dévots, mais personne ne veut être humble.*
Many people want to be devout, but no one wants to be humble.

36 *Le travail du corps délivre des peines de l'esprit, et c'est ce qui rend les pauvres heureux.*
The work of the body frees people from the pains of the mind, and it is what makes the poor happy.

37 *Les véritables mortifications sont celles qui ne sont point connues; la vanité rend les autres faciles.*
The true mortifications are those which are not known; vanity renders the others easy.

38 *L'humilité est l'autel sur lequel Dieu veut qu'on lui offre des sacrifices.*
Humility is the altar upon which God wants one to offer Him sacrifices.

39 *Il faut peu de choses pour rendre le sage heureux; rien ne peut rendre*

un fol content; c'est pourquoi presque tous les hommes sont misérables.

39 Few things are necessary to make the wise happy; nothing can make a fool content; this is why almost all men are miserable.

40 *Nous nous tourmentons moins pour devenir heureux que pour faire croire que nous le sommes.*

We torment ourselves less in order to become happy than to make believe that we are.

41 *Il est bien plus aisé d'éteindre un premier désir que de satisfaire tous ceux qui le suivent.*

It is much easier to extinguish a first desire than to satisfy all of those that follow it.

42 *La sagesse est à l'âme ce que la santé est pour le corps.*

Wisdom is to the soul what health is for the body.

43 *Les grands de la terre ne pouvant donner la santé du corps ni le repos d'esprit, on achète toujours trop cher tous les biens qu'ils peuvent faire.*

Since the great of the earth are unable to give health to the body or repose to the mind, one always pays too much for any good they can do.

44 *Avant que de désirer fortement une chose, il faut examiner quel est le bonheur de celui qui la possède.*

Before desiring a thing strongly, one has to examine what the happiness of him who possesses it is.

45 *Un véritable ami est le plus grand de tous les biens et celui de tous qu'on songe le moins à acquérir.*

A true friend is the greatest of all goods, and of all of them, the one that one least thinks of acquiring.

46   *Les amants ne voient les défauts de leurs maîtresses que lorsque leur enchantement est fini.*
Lovers see the shortcomings of their mistresses only when their enchantment is over.

47   *La prudence et l'amour ne sont pas faits l'un pour l'autre: à mesure que l'amour croît, la prudence diminue.*
Prudence and love are not made for each other: as love increases, prudence diminishes.

48   *Il est quelquefois agréable à un mari d'avoir une femme jalouse: il entend toujours parler de ce qu'il aime.*
It is sometimes agreeable to a husband to have a jealous wife: he always hears about what he loves.

49   *Qu'une femme est à plaindre, quand elle a tout ensemble de l'amour et de la vertu!*
How much a woman is to be pitied, when she has love and virtue all together!

50   *Le sage trouve mieux son compte à ne point s'engager qu'à vaincre.*
The wise find their advantage more in not attempting than in defeating.

51   *Il est plus nécessaire d'étudier les hommes que les livres.*
It is more necessary to study men than books.

52   *Le bonheur ou le malheur vont d'ordinaire à ceux qui ont le plus de l'un ou de l'autre.*
Happiness or unhappiness ordinarily go to those who have the most of the one or the other.

53   *On ne se blâme que pour être loué.*

53 One blames oneself only in order to be praised.

54 *Il n'est rien de plus naturel ni de plus trompeur que de croire qu'on est aimé.*
Nothing is more natural or more deceiving than to believe that one is loved.

55 *Nous aimons mieux voir ceux à qui nous faisons du bien que ceux qui nous en font.*
We prefer to see those to whom we do good than those who do good to us.

56 *Il est plus difficile de dissimuler les sentiments que l'on a que de feindre ceux que l'on n'a pas.*
It is more difficult to dissimulate the sentiments that one has than to feign those that one does not have.

57 *Les amitiés renouées demandent plus de soins que celles qui n'ont jamais été rompues.*
Renewed friendships require more care than those that have never been broken.

58 *Un homme à qui personne ne plaît est bien plus malheureux que celui qui ne plaît à personne.*
A man who likes no one is much more unhappy than he whom no one likes.

59 *L'enfer des femmes, c'est la vieillesse.*
The hell of women is old age.

60 *Les soumissions et les bassesses que les seigneurs de la Cour font auprès des ministres qui ne sont pas de leur rang sont des lâchetés de gens de cœur.*

60 The professions of allegiance which the lords make to the ministers who are not of their rank, and the base actions in which they engage at Court, are cowardly acts of good-hearted people.

61 *L'honnêteté n'est d'aucun état particulier, mais de tous les états en général.*
Honesty is of no particular estate, but of all estates in general.

Portrait of La Rochefoucauld by Himself
(1659)

I am of a medium height, elegant and well-proportioned. My complexion is dark but fairly uniform; my forehead is high and of a reasonable size. My eyes are black, small, and deep-set with black and thick, yet well-shaped, eyebrows. I would be quite at a loss to say in what manner my nose is shaped, for it is neither snub nor aquiline, nor big nor pointed – at least I believe so. All I know is that it is large rather than small, and that it falls a bit too much. I have a large mouth, and my lips are ordinarily quite red, and neither well nor badly shaped. My teeth are white, and tolerably well-set. I have been told in the past that my chin was a little too big: I just touched it and looked at it in the mirror in order to know that it is, and I do not quite know what to say. As for the shape of my face, it is either square or oval: which of the two, it would be very difficult for me to say. My hair is black, naturally curly, and also thick and long enough to make for a fine head. There is something sad and proud to my expression, which makes most people believe that I am contemptuous, even though I am not so at all. My manner is very easy, and even too much so, to the point of making too many movements when I speak.

Here is, naively, how I think I am made on the outside; and one will find, I believe, that what I think of myself about that is not very far removed from the facts. I shall deal with what remains to be written of my portrait with the same fidelity; for I have studied myself enough to know myself well, and I lack neither the assurance to say freely what good qualities I may have, nor the sincerity to confess frankly what my shortcomings are.

First, to speak of my temperament, I am melancholic, and I am so to the point that, in three or four years, I have hardly been seen laughing three or four times. However, I would possess, it seems to me, a bearable and gentle enough melancholy, if I did not have any other than the one which comes from my temperament; but so much melancholy comes to me from elsewhere, and that which comes to me fills my imagination in such a way, and occupies my mind so much, that most of the time I either dream without saying a word or I have almost no concern for what I say. I am very reserved with those I do not know, and I am not even extremely forthcoming with most of those I do. It is a shortcoming. I know it well; and I shall neglect nothing in order to correct it in me. However, since a certain somber look that I have on the face contributes to making me appear even more reserved than I am, and it is not in our power to rid ourselves of an unpleasant look that comes from the natural disposition of the features of our face, I think that after having corrected myself inside, I shall still keep bad marks outside. I have some wit and I have no difficulty about saying so. For what is the use of quibbling about this? Distorting and smoothing over so much in order to talk about the good qualities we have is, it seems to me, hiding a little vanity under an apparent modesty, and using a very adroit manner to make people believe much more about ourselves than we say. As for me, I am content that people believe me to be neither more beautiful than I claim to be, nor of a better temperament than the one I depict, nor more witty and more reasonable than I will say I am.

I am witty, then again, but of a wit spoiled by melancholy. For even though I speak rather well, and have a good memory, and do not think about things too confusedly, I am nevertheless so taken with my sadness that often I express rather poorly what I want to say. The conversation of honest people is one of the pleasures which touches me most. I like it when it is serious and its greatest part is about morality; yet, I am also able to enjoy it when it is gay, and, if I do not say many small things in order to make people laugh, I am still able to appreciate the trifles when they are well said, and I still find that kind of banter entertaining in which some quick and easy wits succeed so well.

I write well in prose; I write well in verse; and if I were sensitive to the glory which comes from writing, I think that with a little work I could acquire some reputation. I like reading in general; the reading in which there is something which can shape the mind and strengthen the soul is the one I like most. Above all, I find a great satisfaction in reading with an intelligent person; for in this way, one reflects at every moment on what one reads, and the most agreeable, and the most useful, conversation in the world is formed from the reflections one makes. I judge rather well works in verse and in prose which people show to me; but perhaps I reveal my opinions about them a little too freely.

What is also bad about me is that my tact is sometimes too scrupulous, and my criticisms too severe. I do not hate hearing people argue, and often I also rather willingly join the dispute; but I ordinarily defend my opinion too heatedly, and when someone defends an unjust cause against me, I sometimes become so passionate for the cause of reason, that I myself become barely reasonable.

I have virtuous sentiments, fine inclinations, and such a strong desire to be completely an honorable man that my friends cannot please me more than when they sincerely warn me about my shortcomings. Those who know me more personally, and who have had the goodness to sometimes give me their opinion about this, know that I have always received them with every imaginable joy, and as humbly as one could desire. All my passions are quite gentle and regulated: I have almost never been seen angry and I have never had any hatred for anybody. However, I am not incapable of avenging myself if I had been offended, and if my sense of honor were endangered by my not resenting the insult that would be done to me. On the contrary, I am assured that in my case, duty would act in the stead of hatred, that I would pursue my revenge with even more vigor than another. Ambition does not torment me. I fear hardly anything, and do not fear death at all. I am not very sensitive to pity, and I would like not to be sensitive to it at all.

However, there is nothing I would not do in order to relieve an afflicted person, and I strongly believe that one ought to do everything – even to the point of showing a great deal of compassion for his evil – for those miserable ones who are so foolish that such does them the greatest good in the world; but I also hold that one must be content with showing compassion and carefully keep from feeling it. It is a passion which is not good for anything in a well-made soul, and it only serves to weaken the heart and which one should leave to the people who, never achieving anything through reason, need passions in order to move them to do something.

I love my friends, and I love them in such a manner that I would not hesitate a moment to sacrifice my interests for theirs. I have some condescension for them. I patiently suffer their bad temper and I easily excuse everything they do; however, I do not show them my affection much, and neither am I very restless in their absence. I have naturally very little curiosity for the vast majority of the things about which other people are curious. I am very circumspect, and I have less difficulty than anybody else not to talk about what was said to me in confidence. I strictly adhere to my word; I never break it, whatever the consequences of what I promised may be, and I have all my life taken this to be an indispensable law.

I maintain a very exact civility among women, and I do not believe having ever said anything before them which could have pained them. When they have a well-made mind, I prefer their conversation to that of men. One finds in women a certain gentleness which one does not encounter among us, and it seems to me that besides this they express themselves with more clarity and give a more agreeable turn to the things that they say. As for being *galant*, I have been this way little in the past; now, I no longer am, however young I may be. I have given up saying sweet nothings and I am only surprised that there are still so many honorable people busy saying some.

I strongly approve of fine passions. They mark greatness of soul; and although in the restlessness they produce there is something contrary to a severe wisdom, they still accommodate themselves so well with the most austere virtue that I believe that one cannot justly condemn them. I who know all about what is delicate and strong in the great sentiments of love, if I ever come to love, it will assuredly be of this type. However, constituted as I am, I do not believe that this knowledge that I have will ever pass from my mind to my heart.

Portrait of La Rochefoucauld by the Cardinal de Retz

There has always been a certain *je ne sais quoi* in all of M. de La Rochefoucauld. Since his childhood, he has wanted to take part in intrigues and this, at a time when he was not concerned with small matters, which have never been his weakness, and when he was not aware of the great ones, which, on the other hand, have never been his strength. He has never been capable of any affairs of state – and I do not know why, for he had qualities which, in any other man, would have made up for the qualities which he did not have. His vision was not broad enough, and he did not even see as a whole what was within his reach. But his good sense – very good in speculation – joined to his gentleness, to his charm, and to his admirable ease of manners, should have compensated him more than they have for his lack of insight. He has always had a habitual irresolution, but I do not even know to what to attribute this. It could not come to him from the fecundity of his imagination, which is nothing less than vivid; I cannot ascribe it to the sterility of his judgment, for, although his judgment is not exquisite in action, he has a good reserve of reason. We see the effects of this irresolution, although we do not know the cause of it. He has never been a warrior, although he was very much a soldier; he has never been by himself a good courtier, although he has always had the good intention to be one; he has never been a good party man, although during all his life he has been engaged in one. This shameful and timid bearing that you see in him in civil life became apologetic in affairs of state. He always

138

believed some apology was needed, something which, joined to his *Maxims*, does not exhibit enough faith in virtue, and when joined to his conduct – which has always been to try to get out of affairs of state with as much impatience as he had in getting in them – makes me conclude that he would have done much better to know himself and to limit himself, as he could have done, and appear to be the most polite courtier in his century.

Portrait of the Cardinal de Retz by La Rochefoucauld
(early 1670s)

Paul de Gondi, Cardinal de Retz, possesses great eminence and breadth of mind, and more ostentation than true greatness of courage. He has an extraordinary memory, more strength than politeness in his words, an easy temper, some docility and weakness to bear the complaints and the reproaches of his friends, little piety, and some semblance of religion. He appears to be ambitious without being so; vanity, and those who have guided him, have made him undertake great things, almost all opposed to his profession; he has given rise to the greatest disorders in the State without having formed any design to take advantage of them, and far from declaring himself to be the enemy of Cardinal Mazarin in order to occupy his position, he only thought to appear redoubtable to him, and to flatter himself with the false vanity of being opposed to him. Nevertheless, he has known how to cleverly profit from public misfortunes in order to make himself cardinal; he has endured prison steadfastly, and owed his liberty only to his boldness. Laziness has, for several years, sustained him with glory in the obscurity of a wandering and hidden life. He maintained the Archbishopric of Paris against the power of Cardinal Mazarin; but, after the death of this minister, he resigned without knowing what he was doing, and without taking advantage of this opportunity to advance the interests of his friends and himself. He has entered into various conclaves, and his conduct always has increased his reputation. His natural bent is idleness; he nevertheless works actively on matters which are pressing, and he rests nonchalantly when they are done. He has a presence of mind, and he knows so well how to turn to his own advantage the occasions that fortune offers to him, that it seems as if he had foreseen and desired them. He likes to tell tales; he wants to amaze with tales of extraordinary adventures, indifferent as to who is in his audience, and often his imagination provides him with more than his memory does. He is false in most of his qualities, and what has contributed most to his reputation is knowing how to shed a favorable light on his shortcomings. He is insensible to hatred and to friendship, whatever care he has taken to appear concerned with one or the other; he is incapable of envy or avarice, whether by virtue or lack of interest.

He has borrowed more from his friends than any individual could have hoped to be able to repay; he has felt vanity in being given so much credit and in undertaking to discharge his debts. He has neither taste nor refinement; he finds everything amusing but enjoys nothing; he skillfully avoids letting people understand that he only has a shallow knowledge of all things. The retirement he just went into is the most dazzling and the most false action of his whole life; it is a sacrifice he makes to his pride under the pretext of devotion: he leaves court, where he cannot find a position, and he withdraws from a world that withdraws from him.

Selected Bibliography

Editions of La Rochefoucauld

Réflexions ou sentences et maximes morales. 5th edition. Paris: Claude Barbin, 1678.

Œuvres de La Rochefoucauld. Edited by M.D.L. Gilbert, J. Gourdault, A. Régnier, and H. Régnier. New edition. 4 vols. *Collection des Grands Ecrivains de la France.* Paris: Hachette, 1868–83.

Œuvres complètes. Edited by L. Martin-Chauffier. Revised by J. Marchand. Paris: Bibliothèque de la Pléiade, 1957.

Maximes. Edited by J. Truchet. 3rd edition revised and augmented. Paris: Classiques Garnier, 1992.

Maximes. Edited by Jean Lafond. Imprimerie Nationale, 1998.

Secondary Works

Clark, Henry C. *La Rochefoucauld and the Language of Unmasking in Seventeenth-Century France.* Geneva: Droz, 1994.

Epstein, Joseph. "La Rochefoucauld: Maximum Maximist." *New Criterion* 14 (June 1996), 15–24.

Fine, Peter Martin. *Vauvenargues and La Rochefoucauld.* Manchester: Manchester University Press, 1974.

Hodgson, Richard G. *Falsehood Disguised: Unmasking the Truth in La Rochefoucauld.* West Lafayette, Ind.: Purdue University Press, 1995.

Holman, Robyn, and Barchilon, Jacques, editors. *Concordance to the "Maximes" of La Rochefoucauld.* Boulder: University Press of Colorado, 1996.

Krailsheimer, A. J. *Studies in Self-Interest from Descartes to La Bruyère.* Oxford: Clarendon Press, 1962.

Levi, Anthony. *French Moralists: The Theory of the Passions, 1585–1689.* Oxford: Clarendon Press, 1964.

Lewis, Philip E. *La Rochefoucauld: The Art of Abstraction.* Ithaca, N.Y.: Cornell University Press, 1977.

Magendie, M. *La Politesse Mondaine et les théories de l'honnêteté, en France, au XVII siècle, de 1600 à 1660.* 2 vols. Paris: Félix Alcan, 1925.

Moore. W. G. *La Rochefoucauld: His Mind and Art.* Oxford: Clarendon Press, 1969.

Mourgues, Odette de. *Two French Moralists: La Rochefoucauld and La Bruyère.* Cambridge: Cambridge University Press, 1978.

Sellier, Philippe. *"La Rochefoucauld, Pascal, Saint-Augustin."* Revue d'Histoire littéraire de la France 69 (1969), 551–75.

Starobinski, Jean. "La Rochefoucauld on the Nature of Man." *American Society of the Legion of Honor Magazine* 3 (1955), 217–27.

————. "Complexité de La Rochefoucauld." *Preuves* 135 (May 1962), 33–40.

————. "La Rochefoucauld et les morales substitutives." *La Nouvelle revue française* 163–64 (July-August 1966), 16–43, 211–29.

Thweatt, Vivien. *La Rochefoucauld and the Seventeenth-Century Concept of the Self.* Geneva: Droz, 1980

Watts, Derek. *Maximes.* Glasgow: University of Glasgow French and German Publications, 1993.

Index

This index is a corrected and substantially expanded version of the index which appeared in the 1678 edition of the *Maxims*. Each entry refers to the number of the maxim; each includes the cognates of the word listed. All of our additions and corrections appear in bold. References to the Withdrawn and Posthumous maxims are indicated by W and P, respectively.

<hr />

1   This is the only entry of the 1678 index listing maxim #504.

Treason *(Trahison)*: **114**, 120, 126, 147, **504**.

Trust-confidence *(Confiance)*: **62**, 116, **239**, **247**, **365**, **421**, 475, **W46**, **W47**.

Trust of the great *(Confiance des grands)*: 239.

Truth *(Vérité)*: 64, **76**, **81**, **127**, **128**, 162, **202**, **203**, **206**, **250**, **282**, 286, **358**, **366**, **376**, **433**, **455**, 458, **473**, **477**, **479**, **481**, **498**, **504**, **W49**, **W54**, **W67**, **P7**, **P11**, **P37**, **P45**.

Tyranny *(Tyrannie)*: 461, W1, P21.

Understanding *(Pénétration)*: 377, 425, **W1**.

Ungratefulness *(Ingratitude)*: 96, 226, **299**, **306**, **317**.

Unhappiness *(Malheur)*: 49, **50**, **58**, **59**, **61**, 183, 264, 317, 395, 420, 434, 463, 485, **W1**, **W8**, **W9**, **W10**, **W43**, **P52**, **P58**.

Valor *(Valeur)*: **1**, **150**, 213, 214, 215, 216, 217, 219, **220**, 221, 365, **W40**.

Vanity *(Vanité)*: **16**, **24**, **27**, **33**, 137, **158**, 200, 201, **220**, 232, **239**, 263, 388, 389, **425**, 443, **446**, 467, 483, **W35**, **W38**, **P6**, **P34**, **P37**.

Vices *(Vices)*: 182, 186, 187, 189, 191, 192, 195, 218, 253, 273, **445**, 380, **W28**, **P3**, **P21**, **P33**.

Violence *(Violence)*: **266**, 363, 369, 381, **443**, 466, **477**, **W1**, **W54**, **W59**, **P21**.

Virtues *(Vertus)*: 1, **16**, 25, **150**, **169**, 171, 182, **183**, 186, 187, 189, 200, 218, **220**, 253, **266**, 308, **320**, **354**, **358**, **380**, **388**, **398**, **445**, 489, **504**, **W28**, **W31**, **W33**, **W34**, **P3**, **P7**, **P13**, **P49**.

Vivacity *(Vivacité)*: 416.

War *(Guerre)*: 7, 82, 219, 504, W1, W40.

Weakness *(Faiblesse)*: **11**, **44**, 120, **122**, 130, **181**, 316, **325**, 424, 445, **477**, **479**, 481, **504**, **W56**, **P33**, **P34**.

Wealth *(Richesses)*: 54, **W1**, **P3**.

Will *(Volonté)*: 30, **215**, 237, 295, 297, **504**.

Wisdom *(Sagesse)*: **20**, **36**, 132, **147**, 163, 207, 209, 210, 231, 323, **W22**, **W23**, **P39**, **P42**, **P50**.

Woman *(Femme)*: 1, **73**, **131**, 204, 205, **220**, **233**, 241, 277, **332**, **333**, **334**, **340**, 346, 362, **364**, **367**, **368**, **406**, **418**, **429**, 440, **466**, **471**, **474**, **499**, **W33**, **W56**, **P33**, **P48**, **P49**, **P59**.

Youth *(Jeunesse)*: **109**, **261**, 271, 341, **372**, **418**, **444**, **461**, 495, 497.

Maxims